PRAISE FOR WILD MAINE ADVENTURE

William Emrich's passion inspired his book, Wild Maine Adventure. With joy and amazement, he tells of realizing the dream of owning a camp on a Maine pond. His love of fishing, living off the grid, and viewing Maine's wildlife in its natural habitat shines out. This is a book about Maine but even more about the rewards of having determination and pursuing a dream.

—Judith Burger-Gossart, Maine author
Sadie's Winter Dream, Fishermen's Wives, and *Maine Sea Coast Mission Hooked Rugs*

Bill Emrich has done something so special. He has spent a lifetime seeking and fulfilling his dream, despite setbacks, challenges, and adventures. With love and enthusiasm, Bill shows us the fulfillment we might find in going the distance. As a Mainer and lover of camps, I read his story and kind words of my state with a smile all the way through.

—Kimberley Collins Kalicky, author and blogger
Away at a Camp in Maine and LivingMaineSeasons.com

William Emrich takes us on this Wild Maine Adventure *as open and casually as if relating his story to a new friend. The cabin adventure is almost a century from Thoreau's, but even without epigraphs, the comparison could not be avoided. Negative events are more than balanced by the fishing, the woods, the view, and the economic shopping at barn and yard sales for furnishings. Extensive illustrations of birds, fish, and animals give the book a value beyond the text."*

—Robert M. Chute, professor emeritus
Bates College, Lewiston, Maine

If you have ever wanted to experience the serenity of a cabin in the peaceful, alive beauty of Maine but haven't done it yet, Wild Maine Adventure is the next best thing to being there. William Emrich's book calms the soul like the crystal waters he describes, and his pictorial journal delivers the wild natural world he loves. Wild Maine Adventure will please your eye, transport your mind, and heal your spirit.

—Bette Freedson, LCSW, LICSW, author
Soul Mothers' Wisdom: Seven Insights for the Single Mother,

Get ready to immerse in a delightful vicarious romp through a man's dream coming to fulfillment. With the glee of a boy anticipating a long-desired birthday gift, the author recounts his trials, tribulations, thrills, and joys in seeing his very own pond-side Maine cabin manifest and in his subsequent immersion in the surrounding natural wonders.

—Donna Minnis, PhD, executive director
Pemaquid Watershed Association • www.pemaquidwatershed.org

We all long for a passion in life; some of us are lucky enough to find it. For William Emrich, his discovery of the Maine wilderness compelled him against all odds to make his dream a reality. His determination to get there propelled him through various absurdities of human bureaucracy and tradition until at last he could enjoy the more entertaining—if equally mysterious—antics of his new neighbors, the wild animals who also called this beautiful lakeshore home.

—Kelly Payson-Roopchand, author
Birth, Death and a Tractor

William Emrich's Wild Maine Adventure *is a back-to-the-land narrative written by a member of that generation who had a later start. His story, told in a matter-of-fact style, is reminiscent of coming to live on the land in Maine in the 1970s. The photos of a house going up are familiar and show wilderness beginning to conform to a human life. Though he was frustrated at all the details, he was happy to be on his adventure at last. He observes closely the animal encounters he has, which shows how little things, when seen so consciously, can add up to a life-changing experience.*

—Linda Tatelbaum, author
Carrying Water as a Way of Life

A cabin up north, a cabin in Maine. Familiar dream? Telling his story good-naturedly, celebrating each step forward, William Emrich writes like a kindly uncle. Whether sleuthing out waterfront land, out-witting bold chipmunks, listening to loons, or negotiating a self-service firewood stand, he shares contagious joy.

—Kathy Scott, author
Brook Trout Forest

How long does it take to create a getaway, a sanctuary, in Mid Coast Maine—including a rustic cabin in the woods on a scenic pond? In William Emrich's case, somewhere around eighteen years. Wild Maine Adventure *is an inspiring tale of how vision, perseverance, good humor, and improvisation can bring about the realization of one's dreams."*

—Tim Baehr, Publisher,
Stone Bear Publications

Who hasn't dreamed of wildlife and the slow life on a small pond in Maine? William Emrich certainly has. Part love story, part how-to manual for those looking for their own piece of the dream (a house on water, water anywhere), his Wild Maine Adventure *tells a classic American story, and in it we get to watch as his dream comes to life before our eyes.*

—Jeffrey Thomson, author
Birdwatching in Wartime and fragile

WILD MAINE
ADVENTURE

WILD MAINE ADVENTURE

WILLIAM EMRICH

Haley's
Athol, Massachusetts

Haley's

488 South Main Street

Athol, MA 01331

haley.antique@verizon.net

800.215.8805

www.wildmaineadventure.com

Cover photo by Peter Eisele.

Building the Cabin photos from pp 17-23 by Darrell Goldrup.

Other photos by Nancy White Dickinson, Ricard Flematti, Christopher L. Hayes, PhD; Sherrie Tucker, and the author or from the author's collection, from the Internet, or from the public domain.

Copy edited by Mary-Ann DeVita Palmieri.

Cataloguing in Publishing Information:
Emrich, William, 1947-
   Wild Maine adventure / William Emrich; foreword by George A. Smith.
Athol, MA : Haley's, c2016
116 p. 17.78 x 25.40 cm.
ISBN 978-0-9916102-6-6
1. Emrich, William, 1947- --Homes and haunts--Maine. 2. Country life--Maine--Anecdotes. 3. Fishes--Maine. 4. Animals--Maine. 5. Birds--Maine. 6. Natural history--Maine. 7. Maine--Description and travel.
F26.E47 2016

for all those people who contributed in
any way, big or small, to the
fulfillment of my dream of having a
cabin on waterfront land in Maine

In wildness is the preservation of the world.
—Henry David Thoreau

. . . if one advances confidently in the direction of his dreams and endeavors to live the life which he has imagined, he will meet with a success unexpected in common hours.
—Henry David Thoreau

CONTENTS

PHOTOGRAPHS

NICE TO FIND SOMEONE "FROM AWAY" WHO APPRECIATES MAINE

a foreword by George A. Smith

As a Maine native who loves my state, I always think it nice to find someone "from away" who appreciates our state as much as I do. William Emrich has written a captivating book about his love affair with my state, and all I can add is: Time to move to Maine, William!

Well, okay. He lives in Florida, and lots of Mainers spend their winters down there, but come summer, we know where we need to be. And so does William. This book tells the tale of his "dream of having a cabin on waterfront land in Maine." Chapter by chapter, he works toward that goal, often short of money needed to achieve his dream but determined to achieve it. And he does.

I especially enjoyed all the photographs, starting with one of William with a smallmouth bass. Nice fish! Eventually, you get to see the camp, constructed without running water or a bathroom, and, really, it looks very comfortable.

I love his story of searching unsuccessfully for access to a nearby pond where he wanted to fish and stopping at a farm where two fellas are standing in the yard. One of the guys, who lived nearby on the pond, gives William permission anytime to park in his yard and get onto the pond to fish.

Yes, we Mainers can be very friendly.

When William discovers yard sales, well, he gets close to being a real Mainer. William waxes ecstatic at finding free stuff, not realizing that Mainers pride themselves on going to the dump empty and coming home with a full load. At a rummage sale, he buys an empty shopping bag for $2.50 and fills it up with everything from a child's Phonics Smart Set to nine antique postcards—of Maine, I am sure.

I've told William that Maine comedian Gary Crocker and I are creating a community college course for folks from away who want to become Mainers, and William can be our first student. But he'll have to commit to staying here for an entire winter.

It'll be fun to see how the camp holds up!

author William Emrich with a bass caught from the
Mid Coast Maine pond he loves

photo by Peter Eisele

the author's vantage point while canoeing on the pond near where he built his cabin

BEGINNING A PERFECTLY IMPERFECT MAINE ADVENTURE

Okay, yes. I'm involved in a love affair.

And it has been going on for years. I admit that, too.

But so far all three parties involved—my lovely wife Silvia (who knows all about it), the very significant other, and I—are all happy and healthy and doing just fine.

I think that the key to such a positive arrangement is that my significant other is not of the human kind but is a very real place, namely an enchanting area of Mid Coast Maine that harbors an acre and a half of wooded, rocky, and surprisingly wild land. Not only that: on the land resides an off-the-grid, unfinished cabin on a secluded pond that provides home to plentiful game fish and other assorted freshwater creatures. This place, my significant other, fills me with such happiness that I have sometimes shouted out loud in thankfulness for its reality.

My love affair with the great state of Maine began when I took a few short trips to Maine from my home state of Connecticut with my parents and sisters in my youth. When I lived in and around Boston in my college days and after the military when I worked for the US Railroad Retirement Board, I took a few more trips there. I realized then that Maine held a special place in my heart. I felt comfortable no matter where I was in the state and had a strong innate connection to the area. A friend told me I seemed to be in my element there, and I think she was right.

But, of course, visiting a place is not the same as owning property there, and whenever I was in Maine, I longed for the opportunity to put down some roots. Here follows my story of a fantasy that came true far beyond my expectations. It continues coming true every time I am fortunate enough to be there.

I can't remember the exact dates, but somewhere around 1997 or 1998 while I was living with my wife and young daughter in Florida, trying to pay the bills and still have a little money left over to cover those things in life that make it so much more interesting and worthwhile, I began the real pursuit of my dream to own land in Maine's Mid Coast region. That was the area I knew best, so I started a subscription to the local newspaper and began checking real estate advertisements for any intriguing properties being offered for sale. The vast majority of places listed well exceeded my price range, but then one ad jumped out at me for a tiny piece of land right on the ocean with no price given in the ad.

"Maybe this is that little treasure no one else sees!" I thought. I quickly called the real estate agent listed in the newspaper ad only to have my hopes dashed seconds later when I was told the high price. Absolutely no way could I afford it even if there were some negotiating involved. However, on the bright side, that phone call established the beginning of a great relationship with the real estate agent, David Kolodin. He asked me to describe my hopes in terms of Mid Coast property.

I expressed my desire for buildable land either on the water, fresh or salt, or with access to water. He assured me he would be on the lookout for anything promising.

A while later, I talked excitedly with Dave about another property for sale, this one part of a farm's big open field with a view of a nearby pond at some times during the year. Access to that pond wasn't known at the time, but the property still sounded interesting. When Dave inquired of the seller about possibly lowering the asking price, the owner stood firm and refused to budge. Again, because I had such little wiggle room with my finances, that was the end of that.

A lot of time then went by with nothing to show for it, but from Florida I stayed in close touch with the real estate agent and kept checking classified ads in the local Maine paper week after week. Then, in 1998, I spotted an ad that sounded too good to be true:

> **VERY AFFORDABLE LAKEFRONT LAND:** Secluded
> waterfront with 300 feet of frontage on a pond. 1.5
> acres. Ideal for a year-round or seasonal home.
> **PRICE REDUCED**

You would not believe how quickly I called Dave and urged him to get in touch with the owner of the property without delay and tell him I was interested. Dave quickly made the contact, and after speaking with the owner, he felt some negotiation was possible regarding the asking price. I made a lower offer that the owner rejected, but my subsequent offer to "half the difference" proved satisfactory. All of a sudden *we had a deal!* Talk about excitement, disbelief, and happiness rolled into one! I was one ecstatic guy. I had fulfilled a dream of many, many years.

You may have noticed one hiccup in the above narrative. I lived in Florida at the time of the sale, and I hadn't even *seen* the property before I said yes to the owner's price. My real estate agent had sent me photographs of the land, but of course that isn't equal to actually viewing it yourself. I did not have the extra cash to fly to Maine just to view the property. I had just barely enough to cover the agreed-upon price. I decided that I would rely on my instincts, that my real estate agent knew what I wanted and would act according to my best interest.

How fortunate that my instincts were correct and that I had found such a person as Dave Kolodin to be my real estate agent. He later told me he was a nervous wreak when, in June of 1999, he finally showed my wife, my daughter, and me the property for the first time. He was scared to death that I would not like it. After all, I had purchased the land sight unseen except for his photographs and verbal descriptions of the property, and that was a highly unusual occurrence in the real estate industry.

So back in 1998, my search finally ended for our own Mid Coast Maine land. However, my family and I still lived in Florida, and I had about ten years until retirement. I realized I would not be able to spend more than a week or two each year on or near the property in Maine while I was still working in Florida. I saw no point in trying to build a cabin on the land if I couldn't spend a lot more time than one or two weeks a year in it, so the property remained basically untouched except for my brief yearly visits with family, relatives, or friends until I finally retired from full-time work for the

City of Tampa in 2009. That's when I came to the conclusion that it was then or never to build a cabin on the land. I decided that if I didn't use whatever modest amount of extra money I had accumulated for retirement to construct a cabin on the property at *that* time, I would probably never again have the opportunity to do it. Life has a way of pulling you in many different directions, especially life with a wife and young daughter, and I had a gut feeling that if I didn't pursue my dream of a cabin overlooking the pond right then, my dream would never be fulfilled.

I called a building engineer that I had had contact with years before in Maine to see about getting started. However, when I called her business number, I learned to my dismay that she was no longer affiliated with the company. Although the new owner Darrell Goldrup lacked previous building-construction experience, he appeared bright, hard-working, and highly motivated with plenty of experience in the property maintenance field. We quickly hit it off over the phone. I briefly described to him what I wanted to do on the Maine land: construct a relatively small but functional cabin on the property along with a good septic system and well while keeping as much of the wildness of the property untouched as possible. Also, I would need to have a dirt or gravel road constructed to connect our property with the outside world. It would take advantage of my right-of-way across my neighbor's land to the southeast.

Darrell sounded enthusiastic about taking on the job and confident that he could accomplish everything I wanted. We agreed to meet each other in the area to engage in more detailed discussion of construction possibilities the next time I could get to Maine.

Four or five months later I found myself sitting at a table in a Maine diner with Darrell. Once again I went over my construction hopes and dreams with him. Darrell reiterated his enthusiasm and optimism about his ability to carry out the project to its conclusion.

Little did either of us know at the time how many pitfalls, struggles, and detours we would encounter along the way. What an adventure it turned out to be for the both of us.

Darrell said he knew a talented builder/carpenter who had constructed a number of homes and other structures in the area. Darrell felt confident that he would be able to secure that man's services to build my cabin. He suggested that I meet with the carpenter in person and view some of the buildings he had constructed. I did exactly that and was impressed by the excellent quality of the man's work, especially since he charged a very reasonable fee for his services. Things were looking up and starting to take shape.

Before I left Maine that time, Darrell and I formally agreed that he would take on the construction project and manage it to its conclusion. We assured each other that we would stay in close e-mail and telephone contact over the coming months because I could not return to Maine for another year due to work and financial restraints. Once again I would have to rely on my instincts that Darrell was an honorable and trustworthy man who would do his best to accomplish our shared goal. And once again, in the end, my confidence proved right!

Over the next several months while I was in Florida and Darrell was in Maine, we did indeed stay in close touch by phone and e-mail. But before I even got back to Florida, I received a harrowing phone call from Darrell. He had gone to the town office to secure the all-important building permit for the proposed cabin and learned there could be no construction on our particular piece of land because it would violate a wetland ordinance.

"Are you kidding me?" (or something to that effect with a few expletives thrown in), I shouted to Darrell over the phone. I was in total shock, and Darrell was, I'm sure, feeling the same. That we could not build on the land had never occurred to me. I probably would not have purchased the property years before if I had known that fact. Without a building permit, I would most assuredly not have a cabin, septic system, or well constructed on the land.

In my state of shock, I briefly considered returning to Maine to see what I could do about the situation but then decided that was why I had hired Darrell—to take care of problems as they cropped up in the construction process. However, I realized that I had encountered no run-of-the-mill snafu on the road to a cabin being built. This particular road had a dead-end sign. I learned that a federal law passed a few years earlier denied construction on any piece of wetland-protected land, and somehow our property apparently fit that description despite much of it being several feet above the shore of the pond.

Town selectmen generally met my calls with sympathetic responses, but nevertheless it appeared there was nothing legally I could do to remedy the situation.

Then, amazingly, a week or two later I received another phone call from Darrell. His voice sounded happy and proud. "Bill," he announced, "I am right now holding in my hand the building permit we wanted!"

I couldn't believe it. Darrell told me he had made a return visit to the town office to talk over the situation again. Another look at the exact location of our property in relation to designated protected wetlands on the town map resulted in a reversal of the earlier conclusion. Apparently, certain areas of shoreline along the pond did fit into those protected lands, but our property definitely did not. Darrell ended up with a building permit and hurried to his car to give me the wonderful news.

Talk about a feeling of relief and happiness on steroids. Darrell and I rejoiced over the phone. Believe me, I thanked him profusely for his extra effort and determination. With Darrell in possession of a bona fide building permit, we both knew that our project was back on track. Although our project was only in its beginning stages, it had already overcome a deal killer.

Over my next several winter months in Florida, Darrell put in many hours of construction planning in Maine. He had to ensure that, once I provided him with the necessary money to do the project, he contracted the right people to do the required heavy-lifting to complete the job within a specified time frame. We needed a road to the building site cut through the woods, a well and septic system mapped out and constructed, and an area cleared for the cabin's foundation. Only then could Darrell's hand-picked builder/carpenter apply his skills to creating a good, sound Maine camp, as Maine natives often call such a place.

Regulations required locating the cabin area a certain number of feet back from the water's edge. New buildings could no longer be constructed right on the shore as they had been for years. In addition, the site for the cabin had to be relatively flat so its foundation would be stable and permanent. Finding a flat surface on that heavily wooded property would not be easy, because a good portion of the land sloped pretty quickly down to the pond. Once again, I had to trust that Darrell would carry out all hands-on responsibilities I had given him, because my finances would not allow me to fly to Maine to see for myself the progress, if any, he had made. Darrell allayed a good many of my anxieties in that regard not only by staying in close touch with me by phone but also by sending photographs of work as it proceeded. The calls and photographs helped a lot and got me through inevitable slow periods of building construction.

Of course, fulfillment of a dream like mine needed funds to bring it to completion. Darrell and I both had very good prior experiences with a particular bank in that Maine region, so I agreed to apply for a loan for the project at that bank. However, my business naiveté bit me in the behind big-time. I knew that I had an outstanding credit score from the major national credit rating organizations and therefore assumed I would not have a hard time getting a loan. I was so confident that my only real concern involved the eventual monthly payment on the loan making such a squeeze on my budget that it would make life a bit uncomfortable, maybe even cause me a few sleepless nights. But I figured I would somehow get through it okay.

I needn't have worried. The bank quickly turned down my loan application. It turned out that even though I had a superb credit score, I did not have a long enough credit history required to qualify for a loan. It didn't matter that I had previously paid off credit cards and loans quickly. What mattered was that I had not done enough such transactions to fall within accepted loan parameters of the bank officers. And when asked what assets I could put towards collateral for the loan, I didn't have any to offer because I refused to put our house in Florida at risk. So, readers, beware. Just having have an excellent credit score does not mean that you can simply walk into a bank or other institution and be approved for a loan. I am living proof of that fact. Maybe you already knew that. As I said before, my business naiveté did me in.

Where to go from there? Once he got over the initial shock when I first broke the bad news to him over the phone, Darrell urged me to ask the bank to reconsider or to try for a loan at another bank in the area. However, I was so irritated and disappointed in the real world of banking and loans that I decided I would not again put myself at the mercy of the financial system. If Darrell went along with it, I would complete as much of the planned construction as possible with only the money I had available.

When I called Darrell and told him what I had in mind, God only knows what he was thinking to himself, but over the phone he was his usual supportive and optimistic self and agreed to my new plan. The amount of available funds I had would in no way fund our earlier construction plans. We had to figure out what we could do and what we couldn't do. Darrell provided me with a close estimation of the cost of each of the four main parts of our project:

- putting in a short but necessary dirt road to the property
- the well
- the septic system
- construction of the cabin and its concrete foundation

From where I stood, based on the figures Darrell gave me, it appeared to come down to a choice between getting in the well and the septic system or having the road put in and constructing a foundation and shell of a cabin. When I say "shell" of a cabin, that pretty much describes what the condition of the cabin would be. No insulation, no plumbing, no electricity, and no indoor walls, but Darrell assured me he would be able to deliver a watertight cabin complete with doors and windows with the money I had available.

Should I go with the preliminaries—well and septic system—and hope that I would somehow come up with the extra funds for the road and cabin in the future? Or, knowing that it was very possible, even probable, that I would not ever be able to get additional money needed to complete the project, should I at least get the road constructed and a shell of a cabin built so I could stay at the property despite off-the-grid and rustic living conditions?

Looking back, I am confident I made the right decision. I decided on the latter choice. I would finally have a way to get my vehicle onto the property, and at a minimum I would have a watertight shelter there where I could at least sleep and eat. Darrell seemed to be fine with my decision and told me that he was sure he knew a good excavator who could cut his way through the boulders and dense woods to connect our land to the main dirt road. And he would talk with his favorite carpenter to make certain he had an agreement with him to build the cabin as we envisioned it.

So there we were. Despite the huge setback of the bank's disapproval of my loan, Darrell and I were determined to press on and make the best of a drastically reduced construction plan. I give Darrell all the credit in the world. He could have thrown up his hands in frustration and disappointment over my inability to provide him with necessary funds for the original plans and then understandably walked away from it all. But instead he chose to go forward with what was left of our shared Maine adventure. I will be eternally grateful to him for that!

I had given Darrell an idea of what I hoped for in the form of a cabin: enough area inside for a bedroom, bathroom, kitchen, living room, storage/laundry room, and a loft. I loved the concept of a loft, which could be used for storage, as a place for a computer, as sleeping space for guests, or whatever we imagined. No matter what other cuts Darrell and I would have to make in the overall cabin plan, I made sure he knew that I wanted that loft. Sure enough, when Darrell sent me formal construction drawings and a detailed listing of what would be built at the agreed-upon price, a loft was included. I was a happy man!

The proposed cabin would be approximately twenty-four by twenty feet and somehow would include all of the bedroom, bathroom, kitchen, storage, loft, and living areas I wanted. Individual areas would be designated within the cabin but without completed walls. The exterior walls, however, would consist of wooden panels due to their relatively low cost compared to alternatives. Yes, I would have loved to have a true log cabin, but I simply could not afford that. The same is true for a front porch that would have made a great spot in the early morning to have a nice, hot cup of coffee while enjoying the view of the pond or in the evening watching the sun go down to the west amidst the trees. A wonderful fantasy, but again not financially possible. Hey, I can still win the lottery, and then watch out!

With Darrell and me agreed about what we could build within the limits of my extremely tight budget, months went by while I waited anxiously in Florida to hear from Darrell about any and all progress in the land of bear and moose (not to mention of lobsters and steamers, too). I learned that, due to a combination of extremely cold winters down in Maine and large, heavy trucks and assorted other commercial vehicles using the roads there, the state's paved roads suffered grievously. Therefore, even relatively major roads were extremely inhospitable to large trucks and/or heavy machinery during the winter.

Darrell and his excavator had to work closely to come up with alternative thoroughfares for the bulldozer and its driver to be transported to the site to accomplish a full day of clearing and cutting. Many days it was simply not possible. Area road conditions severely limited the time that construction equipment had access to our land. Difficulty completing any construction during severe cold and icy conditions of a typical Maine winter caused weeks to go by without any progress. Long delays frustrated Darrell and me, but we really couldn't do anything about it.

We impatiently waited out the long winter months. Of course, when snow and ice accumulation of winter meets increasingly warmer conditions of April and May, the ground becomes a half-frozen, half-muddy quagmire. And so again, conditions in early spring do not, to say the least, provide an ideal situation for carrying out construction activity in Maine.

But gradually things improved, and the day finally arrived when I received word from Darrell that the excavator had completed the road leading into the property. We were getting somewhere! Darrell had already decided on a site for the foundation of the cabin, a relatively level spot with a wonderful view of the pond and yet far enough back from the water's edge to adhere to building set-back regulations. The new dirt road cut through woods and boulders led right to that spot. The road would end at the cabin site, and I liked that. The property had been advertised as secluded, and I very much wanted to keep it that way.

The next big decision Darrell asked of me involved the type of foundation for the cabin. One option would result in a flat, all-concrete foundation. The other option provided for a number of specially made, hollow tubes with one end sunk deep into the ground and each tube filled to the top with concrete. Then, before the concrete dried, workers would insert an iron rod protruding from the top of each tube. Later, those rods would securely anchor the bottom of the cabin to the tubes by being bolted to the cabin's wooden base.

I decided the cabin would have a foundation of concrete tubes, fourteen in all. The tube option would provide an air space between the ground and cabin floor with an opportunity for air circulation under the cabin. Along with the reasonable cost of such an option, I liked the air flow offered by the tube option.

Things really started to heat up—and not just in terms of the Maine weather. In late spring of 2010, I started to receive more and more progress

newly constructed dirt road to the cabin site

reports from Darrell via e-mail and phone, and many times those e-mail reports included photographs that Darrell had taken of what his crew had accomplished. It was an exciting time for both of us. Darrell understandably was proud of what was being done up there, and I loved to hear of the latest steps taken towards the completion of the camp.

Spring quickly turned into summer, and because of some minor but not unexpected glitches along the way, I could sense that Darrell was becoming more and more anxious about being able to deliver on his promise of a water-tight shell of a cabin by autumn. He did not reveal such a feeling at the time, but I sensed the pressure he was under when I talked with him, so I tried not to add any more pressure on him from my end. Darrell, of course, had to contend with so many different factors—weather, his employees, the tight budget. Everything had to synchronize in a positive way so the project would come to fruition. I, on the other hand, had to rely only on Darrell. Throughout, he remained outwardly tremendously optimistic, determined, and focused.

The summer ended. I continued to receive steady progress reports, many containing the latest photographs of actual cabin construction by the carpenter. Darrell helped me understand the steps needed to complete the cabin, so even though I was far away in Florida, I felt as if I could almost see the cabin going up. I relished hearing of tremendous progress made in September and early October. Finally in mid-October, I got the unbelievably good news from Darrell that the windows and doors had been installed and the agreed-upon project had been finally completed. The cabin in all of its primitive, off-the-grid glory stood ready to be seen and used. Darrell had come through with flying colors. He kept his promise despite having to overcome many big obstacles along the way, and he proudly awaited my presence up there to show me the finished product.

Unfortunately, I had to delay my visit to the cabin by several months until the following spring because of my finances and responsibilities in Florida. Nevertheless, I felt just fine knowing that the road existed to the cabin site and that the cabin was ready and waiting to be used and enjoyed. The few months passed without incident until I could get to Maine and meet with Darrell at the site. When I finally got there, he proudly handed me the keys to the cabin. Each of us, I know, felt a great sense of accomplishment!

BUILDING THE CABIN

photos by Darrell Goldrup

*hollow-tube concrete foundation, top, and
a detail of a concrete tube*

bolt-joined joists, top, and the cabin's web of joists

exterior paneling, top, and developing interior walls

joists for the loft floor, top, and windows and brand new rafters

raising the roof, top, and a gable end

roof shingles, top, and the other gable end

livable and campy, top, and, finally, a cabin in the woods

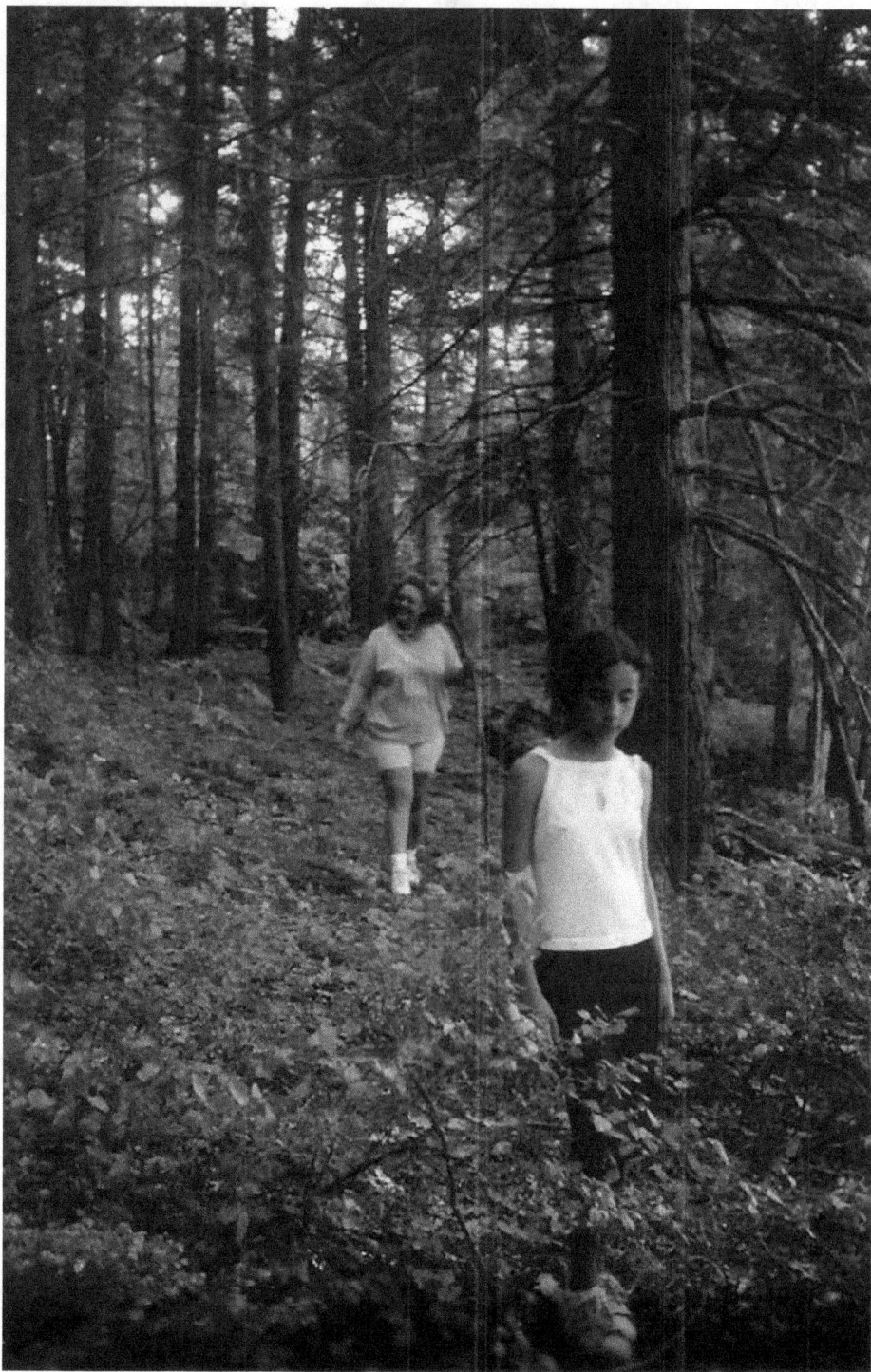

the author's wife, Silvia Abreu, and daughter, Stephanie, during
a visit to the property

movin' on up: the cabin with yard chairs

a very useful donation from the author's wife, Silvia

BRINGING THE CABIN TO LIFE

As I stepped into the cabin for the first time on May 18, 2011 (actually, I had to kind of jump in, because there were no stairs leading up to the door), I marveled at how much larger the cabin appeared from the inside than from the outside. The ceiling seemed very high, and I felt I would have plenty of space for a functional main floor plus a workable loft area. I also liked how the windows let in lots of light.

It wasn't long, however, before my unusual situation struck me. There was absolutely *nothing* in the cabin—not a chair, not a table, not a bed, not a book, not a spoon, not a darned thing. I would have to make the cabin livable by furnishing it from the ground up. It was such a funny feeling for me. I mean, where the hell does one start, especially on an extremely tight budget?

Because I had joined the local YMCA for the approximately six weeks I would be in Maine in order to have use of an exercise track and bathroom facilities, I asked the Y director if he could recommend any used-furniture businesses. He quickly mentioned a local thrift store that offered household items, big and small, at discounted prices. His recommendation started me off in the right direction, and I thanked the director for his advice when I saw him at the Y a few days later.

In the interim, I visited the thrift store and filled my vehicle up more than once with basic living items for the cabin like chairs, tables, and tools, all used but in good condition. I also drove around to yard sales where I had the opportunity to purchase, at oftentimes breathtakingly low prices, many more necessary household items. One tent sale turned out to be a treasure chest. I don't know how many times I loaded up my car with used furniture from that event with hardly a dent in my wallet. I couldn't believe my good fortune. For pennies on the dollar, I had begun to furnish my cabin to the point where it was becoming a home and not just a shelter from wind and rain.

first furnishings for the cabin loft

combination storage room and closet

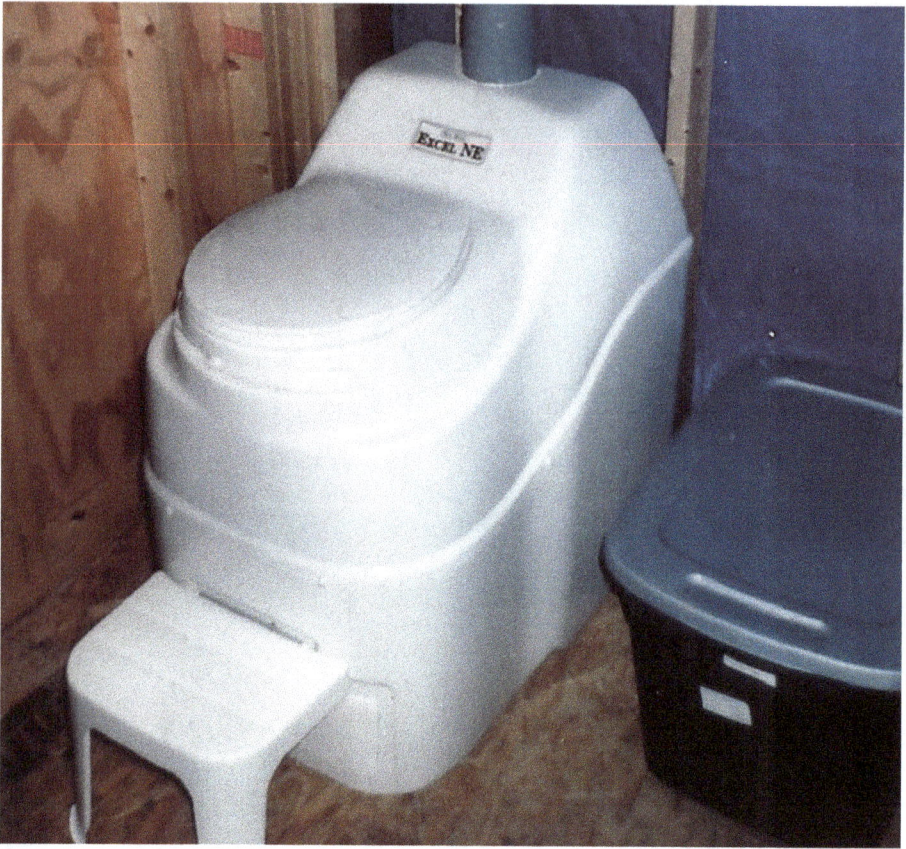

the cabin's Sunmar composting toilet

But there remained a basic item that I insisted to myself I would buy new: a toilet. And not just any toilet. Because the cabin had no plumbing, no running water, and no electricity, I was in the market for a composting toilet. A while back, a friend and I had stayed in a similar off-the-grid cabin rented out by a local conservation organization. That cabin had a Sunmar composting toilet that worked very well. I found a business in a nearby town that carried the brand, so I soon drove over and within minutes purchased a unit that perfectly fit my needs. It was one of the very few items for the cabin that I bought new and at full price, but I considered it a necessity for the new seasonal home.

Then I had to find someone with the skills to install my new composting toilet. Off I went to a nearby home-energy company and came away with a recommendation for a self-employed builder, Clint Smith, who might be able to help me out. Clint very quickly became a valued worker for me as someone I could call on not only to install the composting toilet successful-ly but eventually to put in screen doors, wooden stairs to each of the two doors, as many interior walls as I could afford, and even cut down dead trees that posed a real risk to the cabin if they fell on it. It appeared that Clint could do anything related to building construction and do it very well for a reasonable price. New as I was to the area, I realized I was very lucky to have found him.

When my sister Jean Battelle and her late husband, Peter, offered to give me their old Jotul wood stove that had been stored away for several years, I jumped at the chance and once again relied on ol' Clint to know how to install the stove. He did a great job and then put in stairs from the main floor to the loft in such a way that the stairway was off to the side and didn't take up any essential space in the cabin. My daughter, Stephanie, gave me a moose doormat that I hung on the loft wall, and my sister, Donna Sethi, gave me a welcome mat for the front door of the cabin.

a gift to the cabin of a used Jotul stove and hearthstone

looking at the back of the author's cabin

an early path the author made from the cabin to the pond

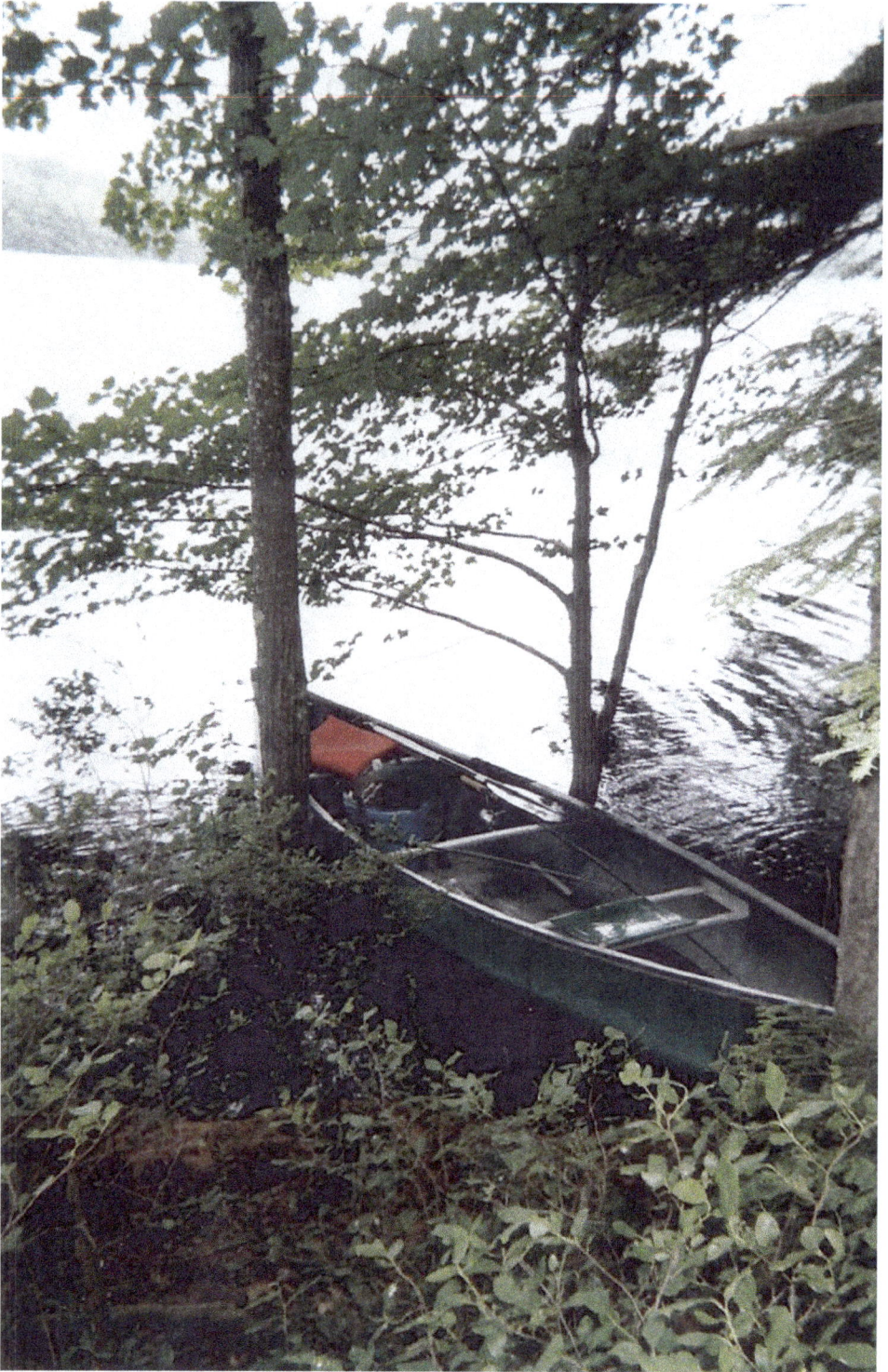

the author's canoe: ideal for exploring and fishing

largemouth bass, top, and
smallmouth bass

ENJOYING A FISHING HEAVEN SURROUNDED BY NATURE

Have I mentioned the spectacular bass and pickerel fishing in the pond?? I absolutely *must* talk about it, dear Reader, because when I first experienced it, the fishing bonanza I found blew me away! Bass have literally fought with each other to get to my lure. I sometimes have had to struggle with not one but *two* bass that grabbed my floating plug. I have even cast out a lure merely with the intention of getting a knot out of my line and had the lure hit by a pickerel as I reeled the line back in. It's not a fantasy to imagine catching thirteen or fourteen nice bass in a matter of two or three hours on the pond.

I felt as if I went to fishing heaven.

top photo from fcps.edu, Fairfield County Public Schools; middle photo from public-domain image.com; bottom photo from gallery.nanfa.orgr

white perch, brook trout, and chain pickerel,
from top

I mean, I was fishing in a pond of less than two hundred acres in Mid Coast Maine. I wasn't in Maine's famed North Country, and I certainly wasn't fishing in the wilds of Canada, Nova Scotia, or Labrador where everyone knows fish abound. I was just minutes from Bath or Camden, yet when I was catching good-sized smallmouth and largemouth bass as well as scrappy chain pickerel or white perch, I sure felt as if I were casting out my line in those wilderness areas.

And have I told you about my love of the resident loons on the pond or the beaver lodge on the northwest end of it? Or how about the deer that appeared out of nowhere on the shore of the pond as I rested peacefully in my canoe a few yards away? Or the otter I startled one early morning as it tried to eat the suet I had put out for the birds? And how about the ruins of an abandoned cabin I discovered as I walked through some deep woods on a point of the pond? All of these adventures and many more add up to an incredible Maine adventure that for me just keeps on ticking.

Moose, bear, brook trout, bald eagles, and loons come immediately to mind whenever nature lovers like me think of the natural inhabitants of the wilds of Maine. Although a pair of moose did indeed cross a neighbor's property heading towards the nearby marshy bogs several years ago, it would be a rare sighting for a person to spot a moose in or around our land. And perhaps a black bear has wandered through the woods or along the shoreline of the pond in recent years, but I have not heard of any such thing happening in my conversations with the neighbors who live there year round. As for brook trout, well, there are brook trout in the streams and rivers of the area, but none, to anyone's knowledge, in our relatively shallow pond.

When I was out in my canoe on the pond one day, I spotted what appeared to be a beautiful bald eagle soaring high overhead, but that was a rare moment. However, when it comes to loons, ah, yes. I see them and marvel at them regularly, thankfully. There appears to be a pair of loons that return to the pond from their winter haunts as soon as the ice disappears every year in mid-to-late April, and their appearance blesses the pond and

a rare sight: cow moose and calf in a neighbor's back yard

surrounding shores with a special sense of wildness that only loons can elicit. I hear them from the cabin calling to each other at night on the pond, and those uniquely wild sounds put the stamp of authenticity on the area as the Maine that so many others and I love so much.

When I stayed at the camp once, every time I canoed to an island, the two loons swam up close to the canoe to check me out. Then one of them, I think the male, put on a dramatic display of diving and water splashing that no one could ignore. Since the display only occurred at one spot on the pond, I quickly came to the conclusion that I was being warned away from that area, probably because the loons' nest was somewhere on the island's nearby brushy and rocky shore. I tried to locate the nest from the canoe but never was able to spot it, and that is probably for the best. If there were chicks in the nest, they needed as much peace and privacy as they could get.

I did notice one thing when one or both of the adult loons came close to my canoe. Fully-grown loons are a hell of a lot bigger than I expected. They are truly large birds with full bodies, surprisingly thick necks, and impressive heads. Coupled with their striking black-and-white markings, their physical attributes make you just stare at them in awe when they are up close. Years

photo by Sherrie Tucker

now and then, black bear

photo by Christopher L. Hayes, PhD

common loon

ago before the cabin was built, I took my young daughter out in the canoe with me, and as we paddled around that very same island on the pond, we spotted four big loon eggs on a large flat rock just a couple of feet from shore. The eggs were fully exposed to the elements because there was hardly any real nest to speak of, and they appeared to be very vulnerable to predators and the weather. My daughter and I did not stay in the area long enough to learn the fate of those four very visible eggs, but I like to think that maybe one of them is the grownup loon that tried to make sure that I did not disturb or harm its own chicks.

Another wild resident of the pond, a beaver, has a lodge at the north-western end of the pond, and it has been there for years. The opposite end of the pond once also had a lodge, but apparently civilization has gotten a little too close for comfort for beavers to inhabit both ends of the pond. If the owner of the active lodge decides during my lifetime to pack up and leave for calmer waters, too, he or she will surely take a part of my heart. I had a quick glimpse of that beaver one very early morning as I drove close

mother beaver with her baby

to downtown to get myself a cup of coffee. As I approached the spot in the road where it crosses over a tiny stream leading into my pond, I saw what looked like a large turtle moving slowly from one side of the road to the other. When I got closer, I realized to my great surprise that it was a beaver. You definitely don't often see a beaver crossing a road, but there it was. It quickly disappeared into the swampy mix of mud, water plants, and pond water on the other side and didn't even bother to give me its famous slap of the tail as a goodbye.

Canada geese also call the pond home once winter releases its icy grip on the pond. Along with the pair of loons, I can count on seeing at least one large family of Canada geese enjoying the pond on any given day. The adults of the species are also prodigious birds. In the spring, they love to fly over the pond while calling to each other with their distinctive honking sounds. They fly back and forth from one end of the pond to the other, making it appear that they are doing that just because they want to and not for any reason of great substance. But what do I really know about Canada geese behavior, other than that I like it?

The geese on the pond are prolific family makers. Every spring, a clutch of Canada geese youngsters arrive, and their parents always appear both proud and protective. If you approach too closely in a canoe or kayak, the parents take quick and decisive evasive action. However, one day while I was alone in the cabin, I happened to look out a side window and was astounded (and delighted!) to see an entire family of Canada geese wobbling down my dirt road one after the other. They marched in formation right past my cabin window and then down the path through the woods to the pond. Maybe they had been feeding in the open fields about a half mile away and then decided the best way back to the pond was to walk right past the cabin. I loved that decision because it was so much fun to witness such a stately procession.

photo by Sherrie Tucker

Canada geese

photo by Sherrie Tucker

bald eagle

Beautiful white-tailed deer inhabit the woods surrounding the pond, and I have had two exciting encounters with them since buying the property. Several years ago, enjoying the day and the exploration of the waters, my daughter and sister canoed with me around the pond. As we approached the northwestern end near the beaver lodge, all of a sudden we heard loud splashing off to our right. As we turned to see what caused the commotion, we discovered we had so startled a deer in shallow and weedy waters near the shore that it took off in a wild panic to get back to dry land and safety. This was not the usual deliberate and quiet deer retreat. This was a let's-get-the-hell-out-of-here-and-fast response. The three of us in the canoe were startled too but so pleased we had seen such a magnificent creature of the forest.

Then there was the time when I was alone in the canoe near the other end of the pond. It was so peaceful and quiet. I decided to stretch out in the canoe as best as I could, close my eyes, and, if I fell asleep, fine. Shortly thereafter, I thought that I heard something or maybe sensed movement. I opened my eyes, and there on the rocky shore was a deer apparently at the pond for a drink. My canoe drifted slowly and effortlessly along the surface of the water and did not appear to threaten or concern the deer in any way. How to soak in the precious moment? Soon the deer had satisfied its

photo by Sherrie Tucker

white-tailed deer

thirst and disappeared back into deep woods without a sound. That deer probably came to the shore every day to drink, but I nevertheless found it very special to witness.

My encounter with a river otter was also an experience to remember for sure. I had noticed earlier signs that an otter was probably in the vicinity of our camp because of a number of opened clam shells in one spot, my favorite swimming hole, in shallow water along the shore of the pond. Clearly some animal had dined on a lot of pond clams. I was pretty sure I knew that otters have a real fondness for that kind of meal. Still, it was all conjecture because I had never been fortunate enough to spy an otter in the area.

You can imagine my surprise and delight when one morning around five, as I exited the cabin, I heard a loud thump to my left. I turned in that direction and didn't see an animal but did notice that a package of suet I had hung from a nearby tree the day before swung back and forth like crazy. Then I noticed movement near the tree, and when I looked intently at that area, a little face stared back at me. I had seen river otters in Florida. A family of them lived in the backwaters of the brackish estuary not far from our Florida house. I recognized instantly that a Maine otter indeed stared back at me. I was incredulous about the encounter because the suet package hung at least a hundred feet from the pond or any other body of water.

When the otter realized I was a human being and therefore a possible threat, it turned and ran. Otters don't actually run in the traditional sense of the word—they lope along in an undulating fashion. It disappeared into the woods. Had our chance meeting ended there, that alone would have been a genuine thrill for me, but the amazing otter added additional drama to the scene by quickly running back out of the woods to stare at me again. And then it repeated the whole run-away-and-then-return scenario a second time. I guess it was as flabbergasted and curious about seeing me as I was about seeing it.

photo by Christopher L. Hayes, PhD

river otter

45

When it went back to the safety of the woods a third time, it did not return. I have never again seen it or even any signs of it around the property. But it is not every day you get to see a wild otter and especially one that, instead of fleeing and disappearing upon your approach, returns twice to acknowledge you and try to figure you out from just a few feet away.

Of course, with all of the young, mature, and dying trees on my secluded property, one could assume that a porcupine would not be far off. And that conclusion would certainly be correct. One day outside the cabin, I heard leaves rustling just above the garden. When I went to investigate the source of the sound, a big, fat porcupine scooted up a young tree. It didn't take it long to climb to the very top to a spot I thought looked like a precarious perch for the plump animal. I wasn't sure the young, thin branches that made up the treetop would hold it. But the porcupine seemed unconcerned about any risk to itself. It proceeded to feed on the fresh new leaves there at its own slow but steady pace. It stayed up in that tree for a long time, but when I looked for it a few hours later, I found no porcupine. It reappeared, however, the next day and even the day after

photo from pixabay.com

porcupine

that, having apparently found a very suitable dining area for itself. I assume that its home is not a great distance away from the cabin, but I have yet to discover its location. Maybe the porcupine will someday remember what fine, tasty new leaves grow on the property, and once again pay me a visit!

I hope one bird never pays me another visit. This uninvited villain of a bird, namely a woodpecker of malevolent intent, apparently saw my cabin as its personal hollowed-out tree because not long after I had moved into the cabin, the wicked woodpecker began pecking away at a side of the cabin in my absence. I only noticed the damage when I went to the back of the building outside where I keep the trash cans and kindling for the wood stove. I happened to look up near the loft window and found a good-sized hole made in one of the exterior wooden panels of the cabin by the disrespectful woodpecker. If the hole in the wood had gotten much deeper, it would have caused permanent damage to that section of the outer wall— not to mention I would have eventually had an unwanted feathered creature as a guest in the loft.

I patched up the outside hole as much as I could and then repainted it in order to discourage the determined bird. Apparently Mr. Woodpecker got the hint and sought other woody places to peck, because I never saw or heard from it again. But geez, wouldn't you think with the thousands of trees around the area where it could hunt for grubs and insects, my primitive cabin wouldn't be the first choice of an industrious woodpecker?

On any given day on that wonderful land (and I am usually able to spend only springtime there), sights and sounds of many different birds and animals reward me. All day long, a black-capped chickadee and its counterpart, a tufted titmouse, frequent the hanging suet and nearby bird feeder with its bounty of seeds. Often a blue jay stops by to harass the two smaller birds and open up an eating spot for itself. Catbirds linger also, as well as a pair of beautiful cardinals. None of these birds likes it when a big crow decides it wants to crash the party, which is often the case.

photos, clockwise from top, pileated woodpecker, tufted titmouse, catbird, and bluejays by Sherrie Tucker; chickadee by Ricard Flematti

pileated woodpecker, tufted titmouse, catbird, blue jay, and black-capped chickadee, clockwise from top

photos, clockwise from top, cardinal and bluebird by Sherrie Tucker; scarlet tanager from public-domain.pictures; woodcock by Charlie M in Central Park; American goldfinch by Nancy White Dickinson

cardinal, eastern bluebird, scarlet tanager, woodcock, and American goldfinch, clockwise from top

One day I looked up the dirt road just a bit, and there, to my very pleasant surprise, was a lovely bluebird. I had never seen one before in Maine or anywhere else. Another surprise sighting for me was a beautiful scarlet tanager with its striking red and black colors. Both birds appeared for just a few minutes, and then, to my knowledge, never returned. And one day as I turned the car into the main dirt road, there just a few feet down the road rested an American woodcock. It put distance between itself and my vehicle in a big hurry and disappeared quickly into the woods on the side of the road. Again, a one-time sighting for me, but to see a bluebird, scarlet tanager, or woodcock even once is a very special treat, and I will always be thankful that I was in the right place at the right time.

Entering and leaving the dirt road that leads to the camp is always a treat for me, too, because several goldfinches inhabit the open fields and swampy areas there. Almost every time that I drive slowly past that spot, three or four of those wonderfully yellow blessings of nature fly around my vehicle. They each add great color to the mostly green landscape and absolutely make my day when I see them. In the same area, I often catch sight of one or more wild turkeys, and it's almost impossible not to stop the car and watch those large birds that have made such a huge comeback in the East in recent years. I have noticed that, in many cases, turkeys would rather run than fly even though they certainly are equipped for air travel. If startled or threatened, they can scoot through high grass with more than adequate speed. And once they get into the woods, it is very difficult to spot them.

I can't say that I have ever actually seen owls on our property, but there is no doubt in my mind that they are there because in the late evening hours or in the deepest part of the night, I can hear their unmistakable hooting. And I can understand why they are around, too, because snakes, red squirrels, and chipmunks all commonly reside on the land. They represent a gourmet meal for a predatory bird like an owl. I am sure that an awful lot of violent activity that I am not aware of goes on in the middle of the night, and it does not involve human activity. It would be the hunting prowess of

photo from bcnature.ca

great horned owl

an owl versus small mammal or reptile, with the owl almost always coming out the victor.

Did I mention snakes? For me they are about as welcome and attractive as those famed piranhas of the Maine woods, black flies and mosquitoes! Even though I realize that snakes benefit the overall health of the environment by keeping the rodent population under control among other helpful deeds, I can't honestly say that I enjoy seeing one. And I can assure you that my daughter feels the same way. One year when she stayed at the cabin for a few days, she turned the canoe over from its stored position on the shore before a short paddle on the pond and a small snake greeted her. It apparently had found the overturned canoe a convenient shelter. Much

garter snake

to my daughter's credit, instead of hightailing it back to the cabin, she managed not only to get the snake out of the canoe but then had a nice paddle for herself out to the nearby island and back. Hey, my daughter's one tough girl.

Another time during that same visit, I happened to look out the side window of the cabin as a slim snake of unknown species shot out from under the cabin desperately trying to get away from a pair of small birds aggressively attacking it. It may have been a garter snake. At first I thought that the snake was trying to attack the birds, but the real situation was just the opposite. The birds wanted that snake out of the area as fast as possible. The snake sought safety in fallen logs and heavy brush of the nearby woods, and the two birds were last seen in that area still seeking out that snake. My daughter and I speculated that they wanted to protect a nest of eggs or young chicks from the approaching reptile, and it appears that they did a heckuva good job.

I mentioned chipmunks earlier as favored food for owls in the neighborhood, but I was delighted they were around for me to observe and enjoy. Most of the time I saw one or two of the adorable little critters scurrying around from place to place on their short legs. They almost always hurried from Point A to Point B when they were on the ground, but they appeared to be more relaxed and content when they were on a branch of a tree or on top of a rock pile. Most of the time when I came into view, a chipmunk ran to a safe hiding place, but more than once, a chipmunk involved me in a stare-down contest. I looked intently at it, and it returned the favor by staring intently at me. Usually I turned out to be the less patient of the two participants, but there was no reward for the little winner except for the satisfaction of knowing that he had stared down that guy in jeans and a teeshirt.

One day, however, one of the resident chipmunks received a very nice reward indeed. I had left the front door open and cabin screen door latched while I drove to town. Gone for a few hours, I returned to the cabin to discover little piles of seeds on several pieces of furniture throughout the living room, bedroom, and kitchen. How those little seed piles got

there had me stumped until I happened to notice a perfectly round little hole gnawed through the front screen door. Then, of course, the whole crime scene made sense. A clever chipmunk had figured out that I was nowhere to be seen. Therefore, since I had left the front door open with only a screen door between the outdoors and temptations of a cabin nicely supplied with food and other goodies, the furry little creature had jumped at the

photo by Sherrie Tucker

chipmunk

chance to sample the fare inside the cabin. It quickly made a hole just big enough for it to enter and exit in the bottom of the screen door.

Where the seed piles scattered around the cabin came from, I am not sure. If the chipmunk had found a way to get into the bag of seeds I kept for replenishing the bird feeder periodically, I couldn't find any evidence to confirm that. Possibly the chipmunk brought its own supply of seeds from outside into the cabin and maybe wanted to find the most comfortable piece of furniture in order to munch away on its snack. As I said before, this was a clever little critter. It had the audacity to come back the next day and stand right in front of the hole in the screen door (I hadn't yet patched it). It obviously was seriously considering coming back into the cabin until I promptly shooed it away.

Hey, chipmunks are not only clever. They are bold little dudes. And despite this intrusion into my personal space by one member of the chipmunk species, I still love to see them preening, eating, and scampering around the property at all times of the day.

Down in the pond, all sorts of turtles make their homes. Often when I go fishing on the pond, I spot a little head popping up out of the water as a turtle tries to see whatever approaches. Those heads seem to pop up almost everywhere on the pond, so it appears that our body of water provides home for a healthy and thriving population of these aquatic reptiles. I observed one modest-sized specimen swimming slowly through my favorite swimming hole a while back. Fortunately, it was not a snapping turtle or I probably would immediately have been on the hunt for a new swimming hole for myself and at quite a distance away from the original.

On two separate occasions, I have found empty turtle shells on the wooded shore of the pond just a few feet from the water's edge. It's very possible that a raccoon or some other deft predator grabbed a turtle in the water and carried it onto the shore for a quick meal. Maybe that same otter I discovered trying to eat my suet hanging from the tree seized a turtle, ate it, and left only the remains. Each of the two empty shells I found on the pond's shore represents a mystery as well as a life history, and probably only

painted turtle

Mother Nature knows the answer to its secrets. For my part, I kept both of the empty shells. In some small but significant way, they serve as a connection for me to that all-encompassing natural force.

As I describe the many birds and animals at the camp, it would be unforgivable for me not to mention the amazing hummingbirds that always help make my adventure there special. They love the nectar I put out for them in a uniquely designed feeder made specifically for their species. If the feeder is red and has three or four fake flowers for the hummingbird to use to extract nectar, in no time at all one of the most interesting little birds on the planet will visit that feeder.

I remember putting out my first hummingbird feeder on the property a couple of years ago. I was very pleasantly surprised when one of the tiny birds came zooming up to the plastic flowers not more than a half hour later. Usually, more than one hummingbird wants the nectar, and several

ruby-throated hummingbird

times I have watched one bird try aggressively to drive another one away from the area. The loser flies away, but not for long. It returns within mere seconds, and the fight resumes for access to the liquid gold in the feeder. Once a bird satisfies its hunger, it usually flies up to a nearby tree branch where it cleans and preens itself. It is such a tiny feathered creature that, even though I know I saw the hummingbird fly to a particular spot on a branch, I often cannot make out its form against the dark background of branches and leaves. But I won't have to wait long to see it again, because within a few moments the bird flitters back doing its aerial acrobatics again as it maneuvers to get more nectar from the feeder.

I have often wondered where the resident hummingbirds have their nests. They can't be far from the cabin because of how quickly they sense that I have put out fresh nectar for them. I would love to see those tiny nests, and that will hopefully be a treat in my future.

On one of my earliest visits to the property, way before construction of the cabin, I was delighted to witness the amazing skills of another fascinating wild bird, the osprey, sometimes called a fish hawk with very good reason. The osprey flies high above a body of water searching for signs below of its almost exclusive prey—a good, plump fish just big enough to satisfy its own or its chick's hunger but not so big that it can't be lifted from the water. Once the osprey spots its target below, it makes a spectacular dive often including a good, wet dunking in order to secure that fish in its grasp. Then, firmly holding the fish under its belly, the surprisingly strong bird lifts the fish out of the water in expectation of a nutritious meal.

On that day, I watched as an osprey flew over the pond grasping a freshly caught fish firmly in its talons. As usual, it had made sure to hold the fish head first under its body to cause the least aerodynamic resistance as the bird and fish traveled a substantial distance to a tree branch on the shore where the bird could eat in peace. The osprey, once among threatened species, is apparently doing much better in Maine, and for that, we can all be thankful.

May I tell at least one fish story? Please indulge me, because I can hardly believe the story myself! As usual on a fine late spring day hoping to catch some giant-sized bass, I was out on the pond in the canoe. Some very big bass live in that relatively small body of Maine water, so my goal was not entirely a fantasy. The bass indeed happened to be biting that day, and I kept one of the bigger ones I had caught by slipping a rope through its gills and securing both ends of the rope to the canoe, allowing the captured fish to swim freely by the canoe's side as I continued to fish. It wasn't long before I caught another big bass, and I decided to put that one alongside the other fish on the rope in the water. So far, so good.

Everything went according to plan, and I was one happy fisherman. But, as every fisherman knows from often painful experience, playing with metal hooks, ropes, and unhappy fish can sometimes make for a bad situation, and on very short notice, too. In my case, as I tried a little too obsessively to get the rope through the second bass's gills, it managed to perform a world-record body flip and land scot-free in the pond. And, in doing that freedom flip to secure its release, the frantic fish's acrobatics resulted in one of my fingers getting impaled on a hook from the lure that I had used to catch that !*%#(#! fish.

To further increase my misery the triumphant bass made sure to let the remaining bass on the rope know that its freedom was a real possibility, too, if it could manage to make a run for it and get the loose end of the rope out of its own gills. Well, I give that other bass credit, because it took the advice of its freed cousin and very quickly swam away into the pond's depths also.

So I found myself in a decidedly worse situation than just moments before. Not only did I lose *both* big bass that I had caught, but one of my fingers hurt like hell and bled badly from the impaled hook. The lure still dangled from the fishing line that hung from the rod, and much to my chagrin, I found not a big fish attached to the lure at the end of the fishing line but *myself.* The hook had managed to dig itself deep inside my finger, so much so that I couldn't even see the barb. Not a good situation at all. And finally, to further complicate an already nasty scenario, the canoe and I had floated to the far end of the pond a considerable distance from our property.

With my one free hand, as my blood flowed freely from the other and I hoped upon hope that I could somehow free the hook, I jabbed and poked at my finger. Nothing seemed to work. I thought that if I could manage to get back to our property, I could then drive myself, albeit with only one hand, to an emergency clinic or to the emergency room at the local hospital where someone would take the hook out of my finger. But the major problem facing me was how the heck to paddle the canoe the considerable distance back to our camp with only one hand. I pictured myself paddling around and around in circles on the pond as I tried unsuccessfully to get the canoe going straight.

So there I was with one hand effectively out of commission hooked to a fishing line and rod while bleeding heavily with no good way to get back to our property. I don't remember if I finally cut the fishing line to free my hand from the pole, but I imagine that I at least managed to do that.

Then, just before I started the painful and difficult long paddle back to camp, I decided to try one last yank on the hook buried deep in my finger. I grabbed the top of the hook, gritted my teeth (and probably closed my eyes too), and pulled on that hook as hard as I could. Miracle of miracles, the problem hook came out.

I was a bloody mess, but my hand was finally free, and to me that was all that mattered. I could barely bring myself to look at the spot on my finger where the hook had been embedded, but when I did, I was relieved to see no major damage to it. I wrapped the wound as best as I could with a small towel and slowly but steadily paddled the canoe back to our land. Upon my arrival there, once I had cleaned out the wound, applied antiseptic, and securely bandaged it, I saw no reason to seek further medical help.

But what a day on the water. If I hadn't managed to free that hook on my very last try, I don't know what the ending of that painful and scary scenario would have been. As for my fishing tally that day, credit each fish with one point and me with zero.

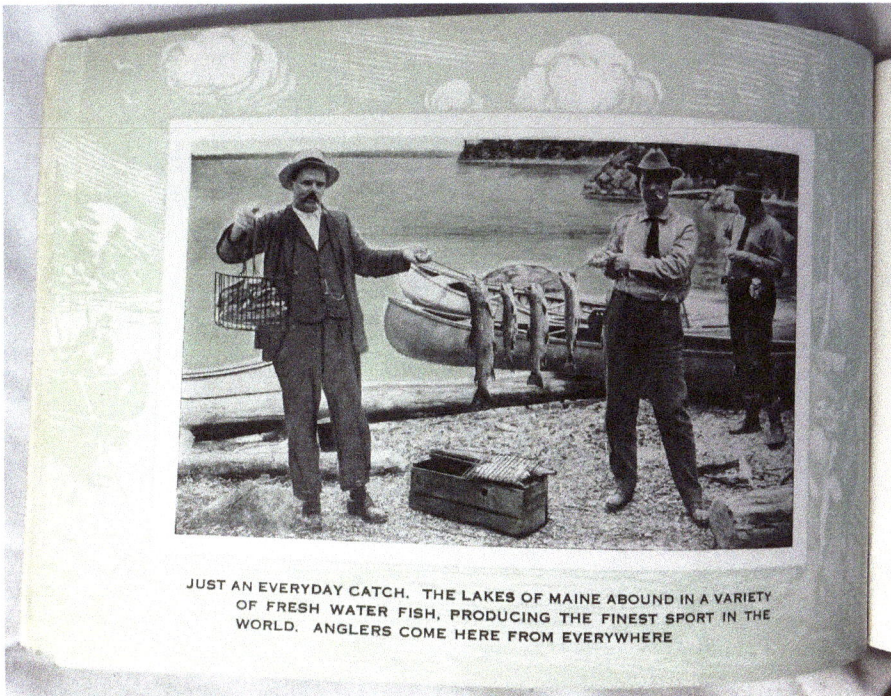

JUST AN EVERYDAY CATCH. THE LAKES OF MAINE ABOUND IN A VARIETY OF FRESH WATER FISH, PRODUCING THE FINEST SPORT IN THE WORLD. ANGLERS COME HERE FROM EVERYWHERE

an early twentieth-century Maine travel brochure
chronicling the abundance of the state's fishery

the author's cabin awaiting a fresh coat of paint

PAINTING THE CABIN EXTERIOR

It was in June, maybe a year after construction of the cabin, that I decided the exterior needed a new color instead of the original combination of dark brown and light brown. I wanted a single color that would blend more with surrounding pine trees and hardwoods. Picking out the new color at a local lumber center was the easy part. Applying the paint to the outside of the twenty-four-by-twenty-foot cabin proved much harder. No problem with the lower half of the structure. The problem became increasingly difficult as I tried to paint the cabin's upper reaches. Getting to that two-story high area with a paintbrush required determination and resourcefulness.

I thought I possessed those qualities until I felt the ladder that I had climbed starting to lean precariously to the left due to its shoes set in ground not even close to being level. Fear and survival mode quickly replaced the concepts of determination and resourcefulness in my very mortal body, and I was very relieved when I scrambled down that tilting ladder to stand safely once again on Mother Earth. Being high up on a ladder, even with the ladder set on level ground, never really appealed to me anyway. When I realized how uneven the ground was on three sides of the cabin, mostly slanting downhill, I didn't take long to scratch off the ladder option and try to figure out a less precarious way of getting the exterior of the cabin fully painted.

Bingo! I drove back to that lumber center to see if they carried one of those long-handled poles for attaching a paintbrush to the top. Relieved that I could set aside the dreaded ladder, I happily drove back to the center, and yes, they had one of those long poles for sale. It wasn't cheap, but it was definitely worth the cost to me because it ensured that both my feet would be set solidly on the ground as I tried to paint the remaining top third of the cabin.

Back at camp, I screwed my big paintbrush into the top of the pole, dipped the brush into my bark-colored fresh paint, and then discovered how flexible such a long pole is. And heavy. I found myself holding maybe fifteen feet of thick fiberglass pole with both hands, trying to guide the swaying rod gently and steadily over to a particular spot way up on the outside wall and then attempting to get in a few brush strokes before either my arms gave out or the brush needed more paint. I almost wasted more paint than I used productively with the extension pole method, but my determination had sufficiently returned by then that I committed to completing the paint job even if it meant I was effectively reduced to a figure of sprained ligaments and pulled muscles. Not to mention a sweaty, stinking mess.

The mighty struggle between man, pole, and paint brush went on for hours, but eventually I saw only a small section remaining unpainted. Such a realization would normally be a cause for great celebration, you would think, but noooooo. The enterprise did not constitute an ordinary run-of-the-mill painting project for this warrior of the wilds, because I ran out of paint. Judging by the few little puddles of fresh paint left in the bottom of the can, no way could I complete that last unfinished spot.

Sure, I could jump in my car, sweaty, stinky, and covered in paint, and drive back to the lumber center to buy another can, but I didn't want to blow another thirty-five or forty dollars on more paint when I was only ten paint strokes away from finishing the job. And then the remainder of my determination and resourcefulness showed up, I must say, and just in time. I remembered I had a small amount of another color of paint stored away. It wasn't the same bark-colored paint I had chosen, but at least it was brown. I also realized that the small unpainted part of exterior wall was, fortunately, barely visible on the northwestern side where I kept the trash cans, dry kindling, and assorted stuff. I thought, "If I can combine the old brown paint with my remaining tiny portion of new paint, it should make a mixture that would, from a distance, blend with the fresh bark color. The combined amount should enable me to finish the project."

Sure enough, the gambit worked, but with no more than one full paintbrush to spare. Once the painted surface dried, even I couldn't tell the difference between the two colors. What a relief! I had completed the painting project, but not before it had turned, as usual, into another Maine adventure.

fresh paint for the cabin

the outdoor shower

BUILDING AN OUTDOOR SHOWER
(AND MORE CHALLENGES)

You may wonder what I do for water in the woods. I don't have a well on the land, and I don't think it is a good idea to drink water directly from the pond. Through trial and error, I have worked out a three-tiered system to cover all of my water needs. For actual drinking water, I buy the least expensive cases of bottled water I can find at the local supermarket.

For washing dishes and cleaning, I previously filled big plastic water jugs at a neighboring town's public water fountain, which I quickly discovered was a fairly common activity for the local population due to the water's good quality and cold temperature. But when I asked our own town's police chief if he knew of a closer place for me to fill my water jugs, I was pleasantly surprised to hear that I could use his office's outdoor water spigot whenever I wanted. What a kind and generous gesture by this police official to a local off-the-gridder. It was one of several positive experiences I have had with local police personnel over the years. Can't say enough good things about 'em.

As to the third tier of my water needs, I raid the nearby pond for watering my garden and other plants around the property as well as for my outdoor shower. Every morning I grab two sturdy, empty buckets and walk down the fairly steep path to the shore of the pond where I dip the buckets into the water until they are almost full. Then I head back up the dirt path to the cabin. Those two buckets provide all the water I need to keep the plants happy every day, so the arrangement works out very well. Bottled water, town water, and pond water combine for a good supply for all of my needs.

You may have noticed my reference to an outdoor shower. Talk about yet another adventure. When I first stayed at the camp for any length of time, I used my seasonal membership at the local Y to satisfy personal hygiene needs. I welcomed those hot showers. But, in my quest to save a dollar in any way possible due to my tight budget, I was very happy one October to spot a complete heavy plastic outdoor shower enclosure offered at a nearby town's annual rummage sale for the ridiculously low price of less than three dollars. A few minutes later, I drove back to my cabin delighted to have that shower enclosure. Months before, my daughter gave me one of those big rubber solar water bags. It came with a hose and spray attachment, and I knew I had everything necessary to put together a shower enclosure in the woods near the cabin.

If only it were as easy as it seemed.

My first decision involved where to put the shower. I had to find a relatively flat surface for it, a bit of a challenge because, and as I have mentioned, most of the property slants downhill to the pond. I also didn't want to have the shower too close to the cabin because then I'd lose the sense of privacy. Still, I didn't want to have to hike a long way through the woods to clean myself up. Finally, I needed to have an area with at least one healthy tree that had a branch at just the right height and strength to hold up the heavy shower enclosure.

The only area that seemed to make sense for the shower with sufficient space not too close to any neighbor's land was in the northwestern section of our property. Plenty of trees of all sizes and shapes grew there, likely offering a suitable candidate. I searched the area and soon found a spot that fit all my criteria: twenty-five feet from a corner of the cabin, somewhat level ground, and a good tree with a sturdy branch that looked as if it could hold up the enclosure.

I imagined just a matter of attaching the top of the plastic walls of the shower to the tree branch about seven or eight feet off the ground and then setting the water bag filled with sun-warmed water into a nice, secure spot in tree branches just above the enclosure. And voilà! I would have myself a free shower facility available any time I wanted it. Things looked very good.

Fortunately, the heavy shower enclosure featured several strong metal grommet holes to attach it to, say, a branch, so I began using several strong pieces of cord to do just that. Within an hour or so, the darned thing looked like an actual outdoor shower, and I began to feel like an accomplished builder. Once the plastic enclosure seemed set and secure, I went to get the solar water bag I had left out in the sun for several hours. It held the expected warm, if not hot, water.

That's when the fun began. Do you know how *heavy* a four-gallon rubber bag filled with pond water is? Hey, let's just say that size-wise, I'm no NFL offensive lineman. It just about killed me to carry that blankety-blank water bag up several steps of a ladder leaning against a tree to place it over the plastic walls. I felt like I was on the losing end of a bout with a Sumo wrestler.

I got the bag up there, but the effort it took to do it definitely did not match the satisfaction quotient of having one quick little shower, so I knew I would have to come up with a Plan B for having a water supply sufficient for a decent shower. Despite the realization, I did have a shower enclosure and water bag securely attached to the tree. Therefore, I proceeded to the next part of the project to make sure none of the soapy water from the shower could make its way to the pond. My inner environmentally ethical self did not want to pollute the splendid pond water about a hundred feet away, so I began my drainage pit by digging a relatively deep hole in the ground around the shower area to filter the water of any pollutants as it entered the ground. I had been required to make a similar filtering system for the composting toilet in the cabin so that any excess liquid waste would drain from the toilet through a plastic tube that went through a small hole cut in the cabin floor. That tube then entered a drainage pit dug into the ground outside.

Let me tell you that any digging in the ground in the great state of Maine is a struggle and a challenge, because you quickly discover that, no matter where you dig, there is very little dirt and a whole lot of rocks and thick tree roots. You can pull out the rocks by hand or shovel unless they are large (and a surprising number of them are). Nasty tree roots, however, feel like stone when you try to cut them with the sharp edge of a shovel or some other gardening tool. I even borrowed my neighbor's ax once in order to get rid of some particularly stubborn roots. But time was on my side, and I finally reached the point where I was happy with the depth and width of the hole that I had dug.

Then I loaded the bottom of the hole with large stones, placing them in such a way that I felt I had put pieces of a puzzle together. Once the large stones were properly placed, I dropped several bags of crushed rock from the local hardware store into the hole. I then smoothed the crushed rock out with my hands to make it somewhat level with the ground. I placed a square piece of latticed wood over the crushed rock so that a person could stand while taking a shower and at the same time allow soapy water to filter through the crushed rock and stones below. Again, I felt a real sense of accomplishment at the completion of the process, and I was ready for the big moment: my first shower, outdoor or indoor, on the property.

I went inside the cabin, undressed, and wrapped myself in a towel. Sauntering over to the shower area, I carried a bar of soap and bottle of shampoo. Entering the enclosure, I felt cold wind just a few inches off the ground from under the plastic walls. Plus the wind entered through the enclosure's only door, which I had a devil of a time completely closing because the little plastic snaps did not cooperate. So even before I started the flow of water from the solar bag, I felt pretty darned cold, but that was nothing compared to what I felt when I opened, for the first time, the spray nozzle at the end of the water-bag tube. *Ice-cold water*, not even remotely warm, greeted me with a shock and a jolt. Very much to my dismay, the sun hadn't warmed the water in that rubber bag at all. It may say "solar" on the bag, but that label did not translate into a warm water supply, and I paid the freezing price.

Quickly recalling my mornings of cold showers back in the US Army, I gradually (and I mean *g-r-a-d-u-a-l-l-y*) adjusted to the shocking water temperature and managed to finish my shower. For sure, it was *not* the warm and inviting shower I had envisioned. A sense of minor claustrophobia I experienced in the enclosure further exacerbated the unexpectedly uncomfortable conditions I encountered. When setting it up, I had assumed there was plenty of room inside for one person, and I had let the walls of the plastic enclosure fall straight toward the ground. *Wrong.* I realized I would have to connect a cord to each individual grommet opening and then pull and secure each attached cord as far away from the enclosure as I could to give more room in the shower for a person to breathe and move. I began to realize that challenges give birth to more challenges in my very real Maine adventures.

First of all, what to do about the freezing cold water in the solar bag? I tried putting the bag out in another spot where it could soak up the sun's rays, but unfortunately got the same disappointing results. Until I come up with a solution to the problem, I continue to resign myself to enduring cold showers.

Then I still had to find a better way to have a full rubber bag of water, even if cold, available for taking a shower in the enclosure. Lugging that incredibly heavy bag up the ladder every time was definitely not the best way to do that. I decided to place an *empty* bag in the crotch of the tree above the shower and then use a small watering can to add water to the bag. I discovered I could fill the rubber bag with water after about six watering can fill-ups, but it meant that, due to the nine-to-ten-foot height of the water bag needed to enable the water to flow downward into the shower enclosure, I had to stand on a stool to reach the opening in the bag. While standing on the stool and holding a full can of water way over my head, I could just barely reach the bag's plastic cap. When I got the angle just right for the long spout of the watering can to release its contents, water flowed into the bag.

However, standing on my tiptoes on the stool and stretching out my arm as high as possible and getting just the right angle was a hit-or-miss proposition. I missed almost as often as I hit. The result inevitably left me getting varying degrees of wet since I occupied the place directly beneath the can. Still, despite many irritating hiccups that came with the new pro-cedure, I was certainly a step higher on the progress scale. I have adopted it ever since.

When I decide I am going to take a shower, I fill a bucket or two with water from the pond and carry the water up to the tree holding the shower enclosure and rubber bag. Then, climbing up on the stool with the can and reaching up high to open the plastic cap on the bag, I go through the process of filling the rubber bag. I allow the can to empty and repeat that step about five more times. When the rubber bag is full, I then make sure that the small plastic hose attached to it heads *upwards* until I am ready to take the shower. Believe me, Dear Reader, you don't want to go through the hassle of filling up the big rubber bag in anticipation of a cleansing shower only to discover in the meantime that the bag's plastic hose went from heading upwards to downwards. You very quickly end up with an empty water bag and a distinct feeling of exasperation. Not to mention no immediate possibility of the shower that you wanted. Do you see why I call off-the-grid living an adventure?

Speaking of adventures, let me share with you a few others I have managed to live through in my patch of the Pine Tree State. Three come to mind that demonstrate I was just plain lucky not to end up in serious trouble.

The first involved a rather foolish activity, namely my trying to push over a thoroughly dead tree not far from the cabin. I assumed if I pushed hard on the tree it would fall nicely away from me and the cabin. Well, as I pushed and the top of the tree started swaying in the air, I heard the ominous sound of cracking wood somewhere above me. Instead of falling down in one piece, the top of the tree must have whipped back and forth just enough to cause it to break from the main portion, and it came down fast.

When I heard that sound, I didn't think I should take time to look up to see what had happened. I high-tailed it out of there as fast as I could. Nothing hit me as I ran, and I breathed a huge sigh of relief. When I returned to the scene of the almost crime, I found a four-to-five-foot chunk of dead wood lying on the ground. If that had hit me on the head, chances are very slim that you would be reading this account.

The second incident involved another foolish move on my part. I had purchased a big piece of flat wooden board with the intention of placing it up in the loft between the metal coils of a bed frame and the bed's soft mattress. I figured it would provide the mattress a good, firm, comfy foundation. The challenge comprised getting that big, heavy board up to the loft by myself. When previously moving big pieces of furniture to the loft, I tied a long rope to each piece and tossed the other end of the rope up into the loft. After getting myself up there, I slowly hauled that item up by the rope until I grabbed it at the loft's edge. Then I secured it.

I don't remember if I tried that method first with the heavy, flat board and failed, but I do know that I decided eventually to try a different way. Not a good decision! I stood on a stool about three or four feet off the floor. From there, I slowly maneuvered the board above my head so that I could, I hoped, shove it just far enough over the edge of the loft. I imagined it would stay in that precarious spot until I could hurry up to the loft, grab the board, and slide it several feet further into the loft where it could do no harm. In my attempt, however, I realized much to my horror that, yes, I got that big board over the edge of the floor of the loft but it then slid back menacingly in the opposite direction behind my head.

Having previously undergone three major operations on my back, I immediately recognized that if I held that heavy board as it fell further and further behind my head, resulting damage to my back could be catastrophic. I did the only thing possible to solve the problem: I let go of the board while simultaneously jumping off the stool and running into the hallway leading to my bedroom. As I ran, I heard a long bang and then felt the end of the board fall directly on the hard bone on the back of my ankle. At first I felt excruciating pain and thought the bone had broken. But when I examined the wound more closely, it looked as if it was just a gash or nasty bone bruise and not a fracture.

After I assured myself that I'd survive, I noticed that not only had the falling board mostly missed me but it also missed hitting the nearby wood stove and kitchen table. Smashing into the wood stove would have caused considerable loss as the stove gave the only source of heat inside the uninsulated cabin. So, all in all, I remained in pretty good shape in spite of everything and did manage later to get that board into the loft.

The third incident didn't involve falling objects but nonetheless had a potentially nasty ending. I had paddled my canoe to a distant part of the pond to try out fishing for bass there. All the way over there I just felt a little weird, as if I weren't a hundred percent. I had felt a little off even when I began paddling, but I hadn't been alarmed. Therefore, I continued toward my goal of fishing and exploring the far area of the pond. Soon, however, I felt the unpleasant, unusual feeling gradually increase within me as I continued fishing. Minutes ticked away, and I started to wonder what the heck was going on.

Right then I should have reeled in my line, hauled up the anchor, and headed back to the cabin. But Stubborn Me said, "For crying out loud, you paddled all the way over here to go fishing, so go fishing." Stubborn Me prevailed, and I resumed casting my favorite bass lure and moved to nearby spots I hadn't tried before. By the time I realized just how bad I felt, I got very worried about my predicament. By then, sweaty, nauseous, and wondering if I had strength to paddle back to our property, I decided to make the effort.

There really wasn't any other option. Not knowing if I would become sicker, I couldn't stay where I was far away from any potential help, so I very slowly began the agonizing paddle back across the pond. Little by little, I made progress and *finally* managed to aim the canoe towards my landing spot on shore where it slid smoothly into the small bushy opening between the water and the land. Exalted Canoe Captain of the Pond, I promptly vomited all over the side of the canoe, an involuntary action that shocked me.

Believe me, all I wanted to do was to get to my bed in the cabin. So I secured the canoe only enough to make sure that it didn't slide back into the pond and then practically crawled my way up the steep dirt path back to the cabin and the very welcome comfort and security of that bed. Several hours later, I woke up, then promptly went back to sleep again for another few hours. By the time I woke up the second time, whatever deep and dark menace had taken me for that nightmarish ride had left, maybe to seek out another victim.

Although drained and a bit weak, I felt a whole lot better. If that was what some people refer to as the twenty-four-hour flu, I would wish it only on my worst enemy. By the next day, I was feeling a hundred percent again and chalking the whole incident up to another Maine adventure.

I would be remiss if I didn't also mention another similar incident mostly concerning a guest at the camp. It all happened before the cabin was constructed. I shared a rental cottage with my dear friend, Ray Fecteau, who happened to be my boss at the time in Boston before I lived in Florida. The cottage is about a half-hour drive from my property. Ray drove up from Rhode Island the day before with plans to drive back within twenty-four hours, so I very much wanted to show him the property before he left. Things went fine until I made the fateful decision to ask Ray if he wanted to join me in a paddle around the pond in the canoe. When he said yes, I was pleasantly surprised, so we headed down to the shore where the canoe was stored.

Ray was a big man not so much in height but weighing in at probably 235 pounds. Still I was confident the two of us in the canoe would be okay. As I got the canoe ready for launch, Ray climbed in and moved to its far end. So far, so good.

All of a sudden I looked up and saw the canoe rocking violently from side to side in the water with Ray desperately holding onto the sides. The more Ray tried to adjust his position in order to stabilize the canoe, the more it caused the canoe to rock wildly. In an instant, the canoe turned over. Ray sailed through the air headed for an extremely wet landing. I could not believe what I saw. I couldn't help laughing up a storm from the bank of the pond. That is, until Ray popped up from under the water and realized that he had come to the surface sans his expensive prescription eyeglasses. I knew he couldn't see a lick without his glasses.

Ray's immediate reaction to the loss of his "eyes" was therefore predictable and understandable. He screamed every expletive he could think of, a considerable number, I found out. I began to wonder what the nearest neighbors thought about the ruckus.

Ray then began a long series of dives into the murky depths to see if he could retrieve his eyeglasses. No such luck. The water was far from clear because it contained a lot of tannins from the endless trees and leaves along its shores. It would have been an absolute stroke of luck if he found those glasses. When Ray finally gave up the search and climbed up on shore, he was definitely not a pretty sight unless you like to see a thoroughly soaked individual in his everyday clothes.

The sight of the canoe lying underwater wasn't really pretty either, so I did what I could to rescue it and refloat it before Ray and I headed up the path to my car. Ray climbed in the back seat and quickly took off his wet shirt and pants while I started the long drive back to our rental cottage on the harbor. During the drive, I remember clearly wondering how I would explain to a police officer, if for some reason I got pulled over, why I had a miserable-looking middle-aged man, clad only in his wet underwear, in my backseat. It would take some real interactional skills on my part to convince a veteran police officer, who has assuredly seen it all, that what he was seeing had not resulted from something unseemly going on!

Thankfully, oh so *very* thankfully, I made it back to the rental cottage without an encounter with law enforcement, and Ray was finally able to change into dry clothes. But somehow he still had to make the drive all the way back to his house in Rhode Island, so I loaned him my spare pair of eyeglasses and hoped that my prescription would at least be similar to

Ray's. Amazingly and miraculously, he made it back in one piece. I doubted that Ray would visit me in Maine again any time soon, and I was right. But, hey. He didn't fire me when I returned to work, so I have to be thankful.

trusty old canoe

EXPERIENCING THE "IT'S-A-SMALL-WORLD" FEELING

We all have experienced, I am sure, the it's-a-small-world feeling. When I am in Maine, however, it seems to happen to me more than in any other place. I once met two separate individuals, each of whom I hadn't seen for years, in one local pharmacy on the same day. In addition, I have found several references in the area's newspaper to two or three generations of individuals with the same last name as my great-grandfather, a sea captain who lived in Islesboro, Maine.

Then there was the time that I anxiously hoped to gain access to a small pond about a twenty-minute drive from the camp so I could try out its reportedly great bass fishing. There was no official public access to that particular pond, so one morning I drove around and around the pond on secluded roads in order to see if I could spot an opening to the water. No such luck. I got increasingly frustrated and thought seriously of abandoning my search when I spotted two guys talking in a farmhouse driveway near the side of the road.

I pulled into the driveway, got out, and walked over to the two men. I asked if they knew of a way for John Q. Public, namely me, to be able to fish the pond up the road. No, they said. Then one of them asked me questions about who I was and why I wanted to fish on that pond. I guess I answered those questions to his satisfaction, because all of a sudden he told me he had a home on the shore of that very pond where I wanted to fish. He said if I just followed him back to his property in my car, I could park my vehicle there and fish the pond any time. I happily followed him and subsequently caught one of the biggest bass I had ever caught anywhere.

My goodness, what were the chances of my finding someone who would invite me to use his waterfront property to gain access to fish when I randomly stopped to talk to two men in their driveway at least a mile away from the pond in question? It *is* a small world, that's for sure.

And just this past spring, as I walked by a cemetery on my early morning walk, I noticed an uncommon last name on one of the gravestones identical to the last name of a family in the Boston area with whom I have been dear friends for years. When I told a member of that family of my find, it turned out that the deceased person in that cemetery, tucked away on a lovely hillside in Maine, could very well be a distant relative of my friends. Occurrences like that give me a feeling of increased bonding and comfort with Mid Coast Maine and its people.

My biggest Maine it's-a-small-world shocker, though, came one day when I went for a little drive to buy some firewood for my wood stove. I had bought firewood at that house before, but since the couple's small business operated on the honor system, I had not yet met the owner. The prospective buyer of wood could drive onto the owner's property and load up the vehicle with as many pieces of firewood desired from stacks of softwood and hardwood located on both sides of the driveway. Then, instructed by a posted sign near the house, the customer entered the house via a back porch. Once inside, the buyer saw a small box provided by the owner for firewood money.

Whenever I followed that simple routine, it made me incredulous that the owner of the business trusted his fellow human beings so much. For the owner and his wife to allow total strangers to walk unchaperoned into their house to place cash into what could be described as a shoe box, a box often already containing cash from other customers, without the couple feeling the need for any security measures was for me extraordinary and inspiring.

But I digress. One day, I drove to the owner's property, quickly loaded up the trunk of my car with firewood, and walked to the porch at the back of the house. When I entered, there stood an elderly man. (Okay, I fall into the elderly column too. Let's just say that this man was probably about twenty years older than I.) As I placed my payment into the box on the table, the man and I engaged in conversation. We talked amiably for a few minutes, and then he asked me, "Where are you staying up here?"

I described the general location of our land. I saw my companion start to grin. When I got a little more specific about where the property was located, the grin turned into a full-blown smile.

"You bought that property from me!" he said.

All I could do was just stare at him. But then I realized David Hatch's last name matched the name of the person who had sold me the land years

David Hatch

before. As mentioned previously, the entire real estate transaction took place between the owner's lawyer and my lawyer. I was way down in Florida at that time relying on an attorney from a small town in Maine to handle the transaction in my best interest. Then, there I was buying firewood from a trusting homeowner's small business about a ten-minute drive from our property when I discovered much to my delight that I purchased my precious land from the same man years before. In my book, that is a contender for the world record of it's-a-small-world occurrences.

It doesn't fall precisely into the small-world category, but one of the proudest days I have experienced since purchasing the land in 1999 occurred when I received an official letter from the town stating that our property has a bona fide town address. I was thrilled. To know that the land appears on the map with its own formal address gave me a wonderful sense of ownership and of being a part of the community.

An official from the town visited me a few days before I received that letter so he could verify that the town records matched the location and description of the actual property. Apparently everything matched, because I received such verification. It is funny how a simple piece of paper with a few words written on it can bring such a feeling of happiness to an individual, but that was indeed the case with me. The letter from the town official resides in a sturdy frame hanging on the cabin wall.

FURNISHING THE CABIN AND MAKING A GARDEN

The framed letter acknowledging my ownership of the property graces furnishings I found at yard sales, garage sales, barn sales, rummage sales, thrift stores, church sales, hospital fund raising sales, antique shops, and any other outlet in the area that sold heavily discounted items. I visited them all. With my extremely tight budget, as I mentioned earlier, I had no choice if I wanted to adequately furnish a twenty-four-by-twenty-foot cabin in the woods so that I could live there with some level of comfort. When I first started to hunt for bargains I sought absolute essentials such as a mattress, chair, and kitchen table.

I brought a bed frame and box spring in my Subaru Forester from Florida. Then I lucked out when I was able to buy a slightly nicked brand-new mattress at a furniture store in town for much less than the regular retail price with free delivery included. The poor delivery guys had to drive their big truck carrying only a small single-bed mattress down the potholed one-lane dirt road leading to my cabin. I made sure that I gave them a tip.

The purchase of the chair, actually two chairs, came from an entirely unexpected and different source. I had been driving around the area, taking scenic pictures with my trusty thirty-five-millimeter camera when I noticed a yard sale on a quiet side street. I pulled up to the house, and before I knew it, I had purchased two matching upholstered chairs for ten dollars each, and a small wooden kitchen table for fifteen dollars—a total of thirty-five dollars for two very nice living-room chairs and a good quality kitchen table. I was thrilled! Transporting all three of those items back to the cabin in my SUV was a bit of a challenge, but I managed to get the kitchen table and one upholstered chair into the car and tie the other chair on top of the car. Off I went, grinning from ear to ear.

Another time, as I drove along a road in a nearby town, I noticed that someone had put a "For Free" sign on a large bookcase sitting tantalizingly in their front yard. Somehow I secured that big bookcase on my car so that the bookcase and I got back to the cabin in one piece. Still another time I stopped at a small yard sale in someone's front yard and minutes later stuffed my car with a piece of furniture designed to hold a computer that has served me well in the kitchen area of the cabin as a good place for storing food items. It cost me only twelve dollars. At another yard sale, I bought a rustic but nice bookcase made entirely of branches of wood for fifteen dollars and also carried away two wooden benches for a total price of five dollars. A nearby thrift shop provided me with a metal chair and a wooden chair for three and four dollars respectively.

And then a rummage sale in the area delivered big-time. If you bought an empty shopping bag at that sale for $2.50, you could fill that bag for that price with as much as it would hold. I am very pleased to report that it held two candle holders, a child's Phonics Smart Set, an outdoor shower enclosure, a small wicker basket, a cowhide tool harness, a wooden toy clock, a cup made of bone china, a new blanket, nine antique postcards, and four small ceramic items. The outdoor shower enclosure alone that fit in that same bag was worth many times more than $2.50, so that rummage sale was a complete success for me.

When I drove one morning over to an island (connected by a bridge to the mainland) that was advertising multiple yard sales, I later drove back to the cabin with a perfectly good shovel that I had picked up for two dollars, a large amount of marine rope for a dollar, a metal rake for two dollars, and a great small wooden barrel for four dollars. When I returned to that island later for another round of yard sales, I bought a child's antique school desk with chair for fifteen dollars. The desk has an old inkwell and pencil holder on top, and the top opens to reveal a storage area for books and papers underneath. I also bought a heavy plastic barrel for catching rainwater for five dollars. Over several months at various sale locations, I bought the following items at astoundingly low prices: • child's life preserver, a dollar

- adult's life preserver, a dollar
- padded foot stool, two dollars
- college trunk, two dollars

- AM/FM portable radio, fifty cents

- wooden rocking chair, fifteen dollars

- wooden desk, fifteen dollars

- twin-bed frame with headboard and end board, (incredibly only) five dollars

- boat cushion, two dollars

- boat anchor, three dollars

- large pail of assorted nails, a dollar

- two large photo albums, a dollar each

- bed table, three dollars

- bird feeder, two dollars

- three bird houses, three dollars total

- large dresser, twenty dollars

- saw, three dollars

- large framed mirror, five dollars

You can see why I not only survived there but thrived. With prices like that available in the area, even a man of thin wallet like me can make it.

As long as I dreamed of having a place in Maine, I had harbored the desire to have my own garden. With the cabin finally constructed, thoughts of having a small garden somewhere around that structure became a little more immediate. I soon noticed an area directly behind the back of the cabin that appeared to be in sunshine for a good part of each day and therefore a nice spot for growing vegetables and berries. Unfortunately, though, that area had been a dumping ground for all sorts of sticks, branches, dead trees, leaves, and vines for the construction crew that cleared out the site for the cabin. Between the cabin and possible garden site lay a fallen tree, a formidable obstacle that would take more than my amateurish woodsman skills to eliminate.

It looked as if it would take a heckuva lot of work to make a dent in that big, dense pile of bulldozed small trees and bushes. It was exactly the kind of physical challenge I enjoy. Time was on my side, and over the next two

garden beginnings, top, and production

days, I slowly but steadily thinned out the tangled pile. It was dirty, sweaty labor but with the exception of the big tree between the garden site and cabin, I had removed most of the pile of woody debris by the end of the second day. I called Darrell who had been in charge of cabin construction, and he volunteered to come down with his crew and cut up the tree with a chainsaw. With that accomplished, I felt as if a whole lot of progress had been made to make that little patch of ground a garden.

Progress slowed a bit when I attempted to dig up the plot in order to aerate the soil and make it livable for my plants. Once again, tough-as-nails tree roots and rocks both large and small made digging even a few inches into the ground a nightmare. I probed possible soft areas in the soil with my shovel and finally found about ten spots that weren't great but at least adequate for what was needed: loose enough dirt to allow me to dig a hole deep enough to host a new plant.

Once I got a foot-deep hole dug in each of the chosen spots, planting of my little store-bought tomato plants was relatively easy. The next morning, I began a daily routine of walking down the path to the pond shore, filling up a couple of buckets with the cool fresh water, and then slowly trudging back up the steep dirt path to the garden with heavy, full buckets. That watering routine seemed to work fine, but during my stay in Florida beginning a few weeks later, the plants suffered. It was no fun to return to a garden of dead and withered plants when I returned to Maine the following spring.

Another year, I replaced tomato plants with perennials such as blackberry, blueberry, strawberry, raspberry, and even one rose bush. Outside of the designated garden area, I also planted a forsythia and butterfly bush as well as several other strawberry plants in other places not far from the cabin that looked like they had fertile soil and good access to sunshine. I am anxious to see how all of the plants fare while I'm in Florida, and look forward to the day when I can go out to the garden area in the back and pick my very own fresh berries.

evergreens near the cabin after a mid-autumn snowfall

Of course, the time of year that I am at the property makes a big difference in terms of doing any gardening there. Usually when I visited the land since I bought it in 1998, I went in the springtime, but after the cabin was built, I managed to drive to Maine in the fall and spend memorable times enjoying the incredibly beautiful foliage of that season. Temperatures were on the cool side but very pleasant until one day in November when a cold front swept through that part of the state and surprised everyone by dropping several inches of snow in a matter of hours. Of course, it was a complete change for me from what I was used to in May and June, and gardening was the last thing on my mind. I foolishly went out on the road in my Jeep the morning that the snow began to fall, and quickly the icy and slippery conditions of the road made for hazardous driving conditions. I just barely made it back to my cabin without sliding into something or off the road completely. But once I was safely back on the property, I was able to take in just how breathtakingly beautiful was the first arrival of snow in the area. The snow clung to everything that it touched, and the transformation of the landscape was immediate and spectacular. I knew then that springtime was just one of four remarkable seasons of the year in that paradise of Mid Coast Maine!

trees and wires down near the cabin after an autumn snowfall

FIGURING OUT HOW TO INSURE THE CABIN

Are you willing to hear about one more Maine adventure? Try obtaining homeowner's insurance for an off-the-grid cabin, and you will then know the true meaning of adventure, Dear Reader. I began my search for the insurance in Mid Coast Maine by visiting local offices representing several national insurance companies. Each agent was eager to help me find a good policy but inevitably came to the same conclusion, namely that no established national company would provide insurance for a cabin with no running water and no electricity. I patiently explained to each agent that if a lack of availability of water in the event of a fire was a major reason for the denial of a policy, our land included three hundred feet of waterfront on a pond, so plenty of pond water was in fact readily available if it was needed in an emergency. Surely a modern fire truck would be able to pump water from the pond less than two hundred feet away.

And it was true. The cabin had no electricity, but I also didn't use open fires for warmth or lighting. A wood-stove fire provided me with adequate temperatures within the structure, and I used battery-operated lanterns and flashlights to enable me to see when it was dark, so I really couldn't understand the refusal to issue an insurance policy. But the official answer was always "Sorry, but no."

Thinking that many people in considerably wilder and less accessible sections of the state must have figured out a way to insure their structures, I tried calling insurance agents with offices located much further north of my area. Two agents up there were sympathetic to my cause and assured me that they would do their best to find a company that would provide a policy for the cabin. Per one agent's request, I sent photographs of the cabin as well as a letter explaining my frustrating predicament, but I soon heard back from her that none of the national companies she represented would agree to provide a policy and those on her list of local or alternative companies would not consider it.

I experienced whatever feeling the mixture of frustration and disappointment combine into. I could not bear the thought of losing my entire investment in the event of some unexpected calamity, especially considering the fact that I didn't have the financial means to rebuild. Without insurance, our land and cabin were a one-shot deal, and frankly, that scared the hell out of me.

At some point, after I received many refusals to insure the camp, my cell phone rang. I listened excitedly as a local agent told me that, yes indeed, she had found a company willing to offer me a policy. We agreed that I would meet with her at her downtown office the next day. The following morning, I sat at her desk and listened intently as she explained that, of all companies, Lloyd's of London would issue me a policy. Lloyd's of London. I thought that was for the rich and famous, not for someone like little ol' me! Moments later, however, when I heard what it would cost to have that policy, I was both shocked and dismayed. It amounted to twice what I expected.

But the more I thought about it, the more I concluded that, after all my struggles to obtain insurance for the cabin, I just could not miss the chance to have it. Hopefully I could find other places in my budget to do additional belt tightening to free up extra money and cover the unanticipated cost. I took a deep breath and said yes to the pleasant and professional agent across the desk from me. *At last* I could sleep a little easier, knowing that my investment and fulfillment of a lifetime dream was protected.

About two weeks later, a Lloyd's of London agent checked everything out at the property and left apparently satisfied that all things qualified. Not long after that pleasant visit, I received the agreed-upon insurance policy in the mail. To sum up my feelings at the time, I will refer to that great old tune, "Happy Days Are Here Again!"

This really is the way a Maine adventure should be, and may it always be that way!

the author near Damariscotta Lake looking forward to more Maine adventures

William Emrich

ABOUT THE AUTHOR

Born in Norwalk, Connecticut, in 1947, William Emrich savors nature in all its forms. A veteran volunteer with the Pinellas County, Florida, Environmental Lands Division, he completed the Coastal Systems Module of the Florida Master Naturalist Program with the University of Florida. For many years, his column, "The Wildlife Side of Oldsmar," appeared in the *Oldsmar (Florida) Community Newsletter*. His photos of the natural world have been exhibited in Florida and Maine.

Bill's visceral connection to Maine may be so strong because, on his mother's side of the family, his great-grandfather was a sea captain who lived and worked out of the island of Islesboro in Maine's Penobscot Bay, his grandmother was born and raised on that same Maine Island, and his mother spent many school-free summers staying with relatives there and enjoying the area.

Bill's career with the federal government transitioned in the late 1990s to his civilian work with the Tampa Police Department. He retired in 2009.

A US Army veteran of the 101st Airborne Division, Bill spent fourteen months in South Vietnam through 1971, where he earned a Bronze Star and an Army Commendation Medal and was honorably discharged with the rank of sergeant.

Bill and his wife, Silvia Abreu of Caracas, Venezuela, have a daughter, Stephanie, and a grandson, Anthony Stir.

ABOUT THE FOREWORD WRITER

George A. Smith of Mount Vernon, Maine, who wrote the foreword for *Wild Maine Adventure*, served as executive director of the Sportsman's Alliance of Maine. He writes an outdoor news blog posted on his website and the website of *Bangor Daily News*, cited by the Maine Press Association in 2014 as the state's best sports blog. He has written an award-winning weekly editorial column for the Kennebec *Journal* and Waterville *Morning Sentinel* for twenty-six years, columns for *The Maine Sportsman* magazine since 1977, and special columns for newsletters of Maine organizations. For thirteen years, George co-hosted a unique television talk show, *Wildfire*, with his friend Harry Vanderweide. They focused on hunting, fishing, conservation, and environmental issues.

George and his wife, Linda, a recently retired first-grade teacher, write a weekly travel column for the Kennebec *Journal* and Waterville *Morning Sentinel* focused on Maine inns, restaurants, events, and activities.

In 2014 Islandport Press in Yarmouth published *A Life Lived Outdoors*, a book of George's favorite columns about home, camp, family, faith, travel, hunting, and fishing. In 2016, Down East Books published George's book about Maine sporting camps, and Islandport Press published George and Linda's Maine travel book featuring their favorite inns and restaurants.

George's website is www.georgesmithmaine.com.

COLOPHON

Text and titles for *Wild Maine Adventure* are set in Avenir, a geometric sans-serif typeface designed by Adrian Frutiger in 1988 and released by Linotype GmbH, a subsidiary of Monotype Corporation.

The word avenir is French for future. The font takes inspiration from the early geometric sans-serif typefaces Erbar (1922), designed by Jakob Erbar, and Futura (1927), designed by Paul Renner. Frutiger intended Avenir to be a more organic, humanist interpretation of these highly geometric types. While similarities can be seen with Futura, the two-story lowercase is more like Erbar and also recalls Frutiger's earlier namesake typeface, Frutiger.

Frutiger considers Avenir his finest work. "The quality of the draughts-manship—rather than the intellectual idea behind it—is my masterpiece," he wrote.

www.ingramcontent.com/pod-product-compliance
Lightning Source LLC
Chambersburg PA
CBHW080052280326
41934CB00014B/3290